45 Pastry Recipes for Home

By: Kelly Johnson

Table of Contents

Classic Pastries:

    Croissants
    Pain au Chocolat
    Danish Pastries
    Puff Pastry Twists
    Palmiers (Elephant Ears)
    Eclairs
    Cream Puffs
    Profiteroles
    Napoleons (Mille-Feuille)
    Turnovers (Fruit or Savory)

Fruit-Filled Pastries:

    Apple Strudel
    Mixed Berry Tart
    Peach Galette
    Blueberry Hand Pies
    Cherry Almond Pastries
    Raspberry Linzer Tarts
    Lemon Curd Tartlets
    Plum Frangipane Tart

Nut-Filled Pastries:

    Baklava
    Almond Croissants
    Pecan Pie Bars
    Hazelnut Pinwheels
    Walnut Rugelach

Chocolate-Lovers' Pastries:

Chocolate Babka
Chocolate Éclairs
Chocolate Croissants
Chocolate Raspberry Tart
Chocolate Almond Braid

Custard and Cream Pastries:

Vanilla Custard Tarts
Chocolate Mousse Tart
Creme Brulee
Banana Cream Pie
Coconut Cream Pie
Tiramisu Pastries

Savory Pastries:

Spinach and Feta Puffs
Cheese and Herb Scones
Tomato and Mozzarella Galette
Bacon and Cheddar Pinwheels
Chicken Pot Pie
Sausage Rolls

Specialty Pastries:

Kouign-Amann
Mango Coconut Turnovers
Raspberry Pistachio Bostock
Matcha Swirl Buns
Fig and Goat Cheese Tart

Classic Pastries:

Croissants

Ingredients:

For the Dough:

- 1 1/4 cups (300 ml) warm milk
- 2 tablespoons active dry yeast
- 1/4 cup (50g) granulated sugar
- 3 1/2 cups (450g) all-purpose flour, plus extra for dusting
- 1 teaspoon salt
- 1 cup (2 sticks or 225g) unsalted butter, cold

For the Butter Block:

- 1 cup (2 sticks or 225g) unsalted butter, cold

For Egg Wash:

- 1 egg
- 1 tablespoon water

Instructions:

Making the Dough:

Activate Yeast:
- In a bowl, combine warm milk, active dry yeast, and sugar. Let it sit for about 5-10 minutes until it becomes frothy.

Prepare Flour Mixture:
- In a large mixing bowl, combine the flour and salt. Make a well in the center and pour in the yeast mixture. Mix until a dough forms.

Knead the Dough:
- Turn the dough out onto a floured surface and knead for about 5-7 minutes, or until it becomes smooth and elastic.

Chill the Dough:
- Wrap the dough in plastic wrap and refrigerate for at least 1 hour or overnight.

Making the Butter Block:

Prepare Butter:

- Place the cold butter between two sheets of parchment paper. Using a rolling pin, pound and roll the butter into a rectangle, approximately 1/2 inch thick.

Chill Butter:
- Place the butter block in the refrigerator for about 30 minutes.

Laminate the Dough:

Roll and Fold:
- Roll out the chilled dough on a floured surface into a rectangle. Place the chilled butter block in the center of the dough. Fold the dough over the butter, sealing the edges.

First Turn:
- Roll out the dough into a rectangle again, then fold it into thirds like a letter. This is the first turn. Chill for 30 minutes.

Repeat Turns:
- Repeat the rolling and folding process (second and third turns). Chill the dough for 30 minutes between each turn.

Final Chill:
- After the last turn, chill the dough for at least 1 hour or overnight.

Shaping and Baking:

Roll and Cut:
- Roll out the laminated dough into a large rectangle. Cut it into smaller triangles.

Shape Croissants:
- Roll each triangle into a crescent shape, starting from the wide end.

Proofing:
- Place the shaped croissants on a baking sheet, cover with a cloth, and let them proof for 1-2 hours, or until doubled in size.

Preheat Oven:
- Preheat your oven to 400°F (200°C).

Egg Wash:
- Beat the egg with water and brush it over the croissants for a golden finish.

Bake:
- Bake for 15-20 minutes, or until the croissants are golden brown and flaky.

Cool and Enjoy:
- Allow the croissants to cool on a wire rack before enjoying them.

These homemade croissants are buttery, flaky, and incredibly delicious. Enjoy them with your favorite jam or simply as they are!

Pain au Chocolat

Ingredients:

For the Dough:

- 1 1/4 cups (300 ml) warm milk
- 2 tablespoons active dry yeast
- 1/4 cup (50g) granulated sugar
- 3 1/2 cups (450g) all-purpose flour, plus extra for dusting
- 1 teaspoon salt
- 1 cup (2 sticks or 225g) unsalted butter, cold

For the Butter Block:

- 1 cup (2 sticks or 225g) unsalted butter, cold

For the Chocolate Filling:

- Dark chocolate bars, cut into small rectangles

For Egg Wash:

- 1 egg
- 1 tablespoon water

Instructions:

Making the Dough:

Activate Yeast:
- In a bowl, combine warm milk, active dry yeast, and sugar. Let it sit for about 5-10 minutes until it becomes frothy.

Prepare Flour Mixture:
- In a large mixing bowl, combine the flour and salt. Make a well in the center and pour in the yeast mixture. Mix until a dough forms.

Knead the Dough:
- Turn the dough out onto a floured surface and knead for about 5-7 minutes, or until it becomes smooth and elastic.

Chill the Dough:

- Wrap the dough in plastic wrap and refrigerate for at least 1 hour or overnight.

Making the Butter Block:

Prepare Butter:
- Place the cold butter between two sheets of parchment paper. Using a rolling pin, pound and roll the butter into a rectangle, approximately 1/2 inch thick.

Chill Butter:
- Place the butter block in the refrigerator for about 30 minutes.

Laminate the Dough:

Roll and Fold:
- Roll out the chilled dough on a floured surface into a rectangle. Place the chilled butter block in the center of the dough. Fold the dough over the butter, sealing the edges.

First Turn:
- Roll out the dough into a rectangle again, then fold it into thirds like a letter. This is the first turn. Chill for 30 minutes.

Repeat Turns:
- Repeat the rolling and folding process (second and third turns). Chill the dough for 30 minutes between each turn.

Final Chill:
- After the last turn, chill the dough for at least 1 hour or overnight.

Shaping Pain au Chocolat:

Roll and Cut:
- Roll out the laminated dough into a large rectangle. Cut it into smaller rectangles.

Place Chocolate:
- Place a piece of dark chocolate at one end of each rectangle.

Roll and Seal:
- Roll the dough over the chocolate, sealing the edges.

Proofing:
- Place the shaped Pain au Chocolat on a baking sheet, cover with a cloth, and let them proof for 1-2 hours, or until doubled in size.

Preheat Oven:
- Preheat your oven to 400°F (200°C).

Egg Wash:
- Beat the egg with water and brush it over the Pain au Chocolat for a golden finish.

Bake:
- Bake for 15-20 minutes, or until the pastries are golden brown and flaky.

Cool and Enjoy:
- Allow the Pain au Chocolat to cool on a wire rack before enjoying.

These homemade Pain au Chocolat are a delightful treat with layers of buttery, flaky pastry and a gooey chocolate center. Enjoy them with a cup of coffee for a perfect French breakfast experience!

Danish Pastries

Ingredients:

For the Dough:

- 1 1/4 cups (300 ml) warm milk
- 2 tablespoons active dry yeast
- 1/4 cup (50g) granulated sugar
- 3 1/2 cups (450g) all-purpose flour, plus extra for dusting
- 1 teaspoon salt
- 1 cup (2 sticks or 225g) unsalted butter, cold

For the Filling:

- Fruit preserves (apricot, raspberry, etc.)
- Cream cheese filling (mix cream cheese with sugar and vanilla extract)

For the Glaze:

- 1/2 cup (60g) powdered sugar
- 1-2 tablespoons milk
- 1/2 teaspoon vanilla extract

Instructions:

Making the Dough:

    Activate Yeast:
- In a bowl, combine warm milk, active dry yeast, and sugar. Let it sit for about 5-10 minutes until it becomes frothy.

    Prepare Flour Mixture:
- In a large mixing bowl, combine the flour and salt. Make a well in the center and pour in the yeast mixture. Mix until a dough forms.

    Knead the Dough:
- Turn the dough out onto a floured surface and knead for about 5-7 minutes, or until it becomes smooth and elastic.

    Chill the Dough:
- Wrap the dough in plastic wrap and refrigerate for at least 1 hour or overnight.

Making the Butter Block:

- Prepare Butter:
  - Place the cold butter between two sheets of parchment paper. Using a rolling pin, pound and roll the butter into a rectangle, approximately 1/2 inch thick.
- Chill Butter:
  - Place the butter block in the refrigerator for about 30 minutes.

Laminate the Dough:

- Roll and Fold:
  - Roll out the chilled dough on a floured surface into a rectangle. Place the chilled butter block in the center of the dough. Fold the dough over the butter, sealing the edges.
- First Turn:
  - Roll out the dough into a rectangle again, then fold it into thirds like a letter. This is the first turn. Chill for 30 minutes.
- Repeat Turns:
  - Repeat the rolling and folding process (second and third turns). Chill the dough for 30 minutes between each turn.
- Final Chill:
  - After the last turn, chill the dough for at least 1 hour or overnight.

Shaping Danish Pastries:

- Roll and Cut:
  - Roll out the laminated dough into a large rectangle. Cut it into smaller squares or rectangles.
- Create Wells:
  - Using a knife, make small cuts along the edges of each piece to create a well for the filling.
- Add Filling:
  - Place a spoonful of fruit preserves or cream cheese filling in the center of each pastry.
- Shape:
  - Fold the corners of each pastry towards the center, creating a pinwheel shape.
- Proofing:
  - Place the shaped Danish pastries on a baking sheet, cover with a cloth, and let them proof for 1-2 hours, or until doubled in size.

Preheat Oven:
- Preheat your oven to 400°F (200°C).

Bake:
- Bake for 15-20 minutes, or until the pastries are golden brown and flaky.

Making the Glaze:

Prepare Glaze:
- In a bowl, whisk together powdered sugar, milk, and vanilla extract until smooth.

Glaze Pastries:
- Once the Danish pastries have cooled slightly, drizzle the glaze over the top.

Serve and Enjoy:
- Allow the Danish pastries to cool completely before serving.

These homemade Danish pastries are a delightful treat with a buttery and flaky texture. Customize the fillings and enjoy these pastries with a cup of coffee or tea.

Puff Pastry Twists

Ingredients:

- 1 sheet of puff pastry, thawed if frozen
- 1 egg (for egg wash)
- Optional toppings:
    - Grated Parmesan cheese
    - Sesame seeds
    - Poppy seeds
    - Paprika
    - Dried herbs (such as thyme or rosemary)

Instructions:

Preheat the Oven:
- Preheat your oven to the temperature specified on the puff pastry package (usually around 400°F or 200°C).

Roll Out Puff Pastry:
- On a lightly floured surface, roll out the puff pastry sheet to smooth out any creases.

Optional Seasoning:
- If you want to add extra flavor, sprinkle grated Parmesan cheese, sesame seeds, poppy seeds, paprika, or dried herbs evenly over the puff pastry sheet.

Fold the Puff Pastry:
- Fold the puff pastry sheet in half lengthwise to create a double layer.

Cut into Strips:
- Using a sharp knife or a pizza cutter, cut the puff pastry into strips, about 1/2 to 1 inch wide.

Twist the Strips:
- Twist each strip by holding both ends and turning in opposite directions. This will create a spiral twist.

Egg Wash:
- In a small bowl, beat the egg. Brush the twists with the beaten egg to give them a golden color when baked.

Bake:
- Place the twisted puff pastry strips on a baking sheet lined with parchment paper. Bake in the preheated oven according to the puff pastry package instructions or until the twists are golden brown and puffed up.

Cool and Serve:
- Allow the puff pastry twists to cool slightly before serving. They can be enjoyed warm or at room temperature.

Optional Dipping Sauce:
- Serve the twists with your favorite dipping sauce, such as marinara sauce, pesto, or mustard.

These puff pastry twists are not only delicious but also versatile. You can experiment with different seasonings and toppings to create a variety of flavors. Enjoy them as a quick snack, appetizer, or party treat!

Palmiers (Elephant Ears)

Ingredients:

- 1 sheet of puff pastry, thawed if frozen
- 1 egg (for egg wash)
- Optional toppings:
    - Grated Parmesan cheese
    - Sesame seeds
    - Poppy seeds
    - Paprika
    - Dried herbs (such as thyme or rosemary)

Instructions:

Preheat the Oven:
- Preheat your oven to the temperature specified on the puff pastry package (usually around 400°F or 200°C).

Roll Out Puff Pastry:
- On a lightly floured surface, roll out the puff pastry sheet to smooth out any creases.

Optional Seasoning:
- If you want to add extra flavor, sprinkle grated Parmesan cheese, sesame seeds, poppy seeds, paprika, or dried herbs evenly over the puff pastry sheet.

Fold the Puff Pastry:
- Fold the puff pastry sheet in half lengthwise to create a double layer.

Cut into Strips:
- Using a sharp knife or a pizza cutter, cut the puff pastry into strips, about 1/2 to 1 inch wide.

Twist the Strips:
- Twist each strip by holding both ends and turning in opposite directions. This will create a spiral twist.

Egg Wash:
- In a small bowl, beat the egg. Brush the twists with the beaten egg to give them a golden color when baked.

Bake:
- Place the twisted puff pastry strips on a baking sheet lined with parchment paper. Bake in the preheated oven according to the puff pastry package instructions or until the twists are golden brown and puffed up.

Cool and Serve:
- Allow the puff pastry twists to cool slightly before serving. They can be enjoyed warm or at room temperature.

Optional Dipping Sauce:
- Serve the twists with your favorite dipping sauce, such as marinara sauce, pesto, or mustard.

These puff pastry twists are not only delicious but also versatile. You can experiment with different seasonings and toppings to create a variety of flavors. Enjoy them as a quick snack, appetizer, or party treat!

Eclairs

Ingredients:

For the Choux Pastry:

- 1/2 cup (1 stick or 113g) unsalted butter
- 1 cup (240ml) water
- 1 cup (125g) all-purpose flour
- 1/4 teaspoon salt
- 4 large eggs

For the Filling:

- 2 cups (480ml) whole milk
- 4 large egg yolks
- 1/2 cup (100g) granulated sugar
- 1/3 cup (40g) cornstarch
- 1 teaspoon vanilla extract

For the Chocolate Glaze:

- 4 ounces (120g) dark chocolate, chopped
- 1/2 cup (120ml) heavy cream
- 2 tablespoons (30g) unsalted butter
- 1 cup (120g) powdered sugar (optional, for additional sweetness)

Instructions:

Making the Choux Pastry:

Preheat the Oven:
- Preheat your oven to 425°F (220°C). Line a baking sheet with parchment paper.

Prepare the Dough:
- In a saucepan, combine butter, water, and salt. Bring to a boil. Remove from heat and add flour all at once. Stir vigorously until the mixture forms a ball.

Add Eggs:
- Add eggs one at a time, beating well after each addition. The dough should be smooth and glossy.

Pipe Éclairs:
- Transfer the choux pastry dough to a piping bag fitted with a large round tip. Pipe 4-5 inch long strips onto the prepared baking sheet, leaving space between each éclair.

Bake:
- Bake in the preheated oven for 15 minutes, then reduce the temperature to 375°F (190°C) and continue baking for an additional 10-15 minutes or until the éclairs are golden brown and puffed.

Cool:
- Allow the éclairs to cool completely on a wire rack.

Making the Filling:

Prepare Custard:
- In a saucepan, heat the milk until it just begins to simmer. In a separate bowl, whisk together egg yolks, sugar, and cornstarch until well combined.

Temper Eggs:
- Gradually whisk the hot milk into the egg mixture to temper the eggs. Return the mixture to the saucepan and cook over medium heat, stirring constantly, until it thickens into a custard-like consistency.

Add Vanilla:
- Remove from heat and stir in vanilla extract. Allow the custard to cool.

Fill Éclairs:
- Cut a small slit into the side of each éclair and pipe or spoon the custard into the hollow cavity.

Making the Chocolate Glaze:

Melt Chocolate:
- In a heatproof bowl, melt the chopped dark chocolate with heavy cream over a double boiler or in the microwave, stirring until smooth.

Add Butter:
- Stir in butter until fully melted. Optionally, whisk in powdered sugar for additional sweetness.

Glaze Éclairs:
- Dip the top of each éclair into the chocolate glaze, allowing any excess to drip off.

Chill:
- Place the glazed éclairs in the refrigerator for the chocolate glaze to set.

Serve and Enjoy:

- Once the chocolate glaze has set, your éclairs are ready to be served. Enjoy these delicious homemade treats!

These chocolate éclairs are a delightful combination of crisp pastry, creamy custard filling, and rich chocolate glaze. They are sure to impress at any dessert table or special occasion.

Cream Puffs

Ingredients:

For the Choux Pastry:

- 1/2 cup (1 stick or 113g) unsalted butter
- 1 cup (240ml) water
- 1 cup (125g) all-purpose flour
- 1/4 teaspoon salt
- 4 large eggs

For the Whipped Cream Filling:

- 2 cups (480ml) heavy cream
- 1/2 cup (60g) powdered sugar
- 1 teaspoon vanilla extract

For the Chocolate Ganache (Optional):

- 4 ounces (120g) dark chocolate, chopped
- 1/2 cup (120ml) heavy cream
- 2 tablespoons (30g) unsalted butter

Instructions:

Making the Choux Pastry:

Preheat the Oven:
- Preheat your oven to 425°F (220°C). Line a baking sheet with parchment paper.

Prepare the Dough:
- In a saucepan, combine butter, water, and salt. Bring to a boil. Remove from heat and add flour all at once. Stir vigorously until the mixture forms a ball.

Add Eggs:
- Add eggs one at a time, beating well after each addition. The dough should be smooth and glossy.

Pipe Puffs:

- Transfer the choux pastry dough to a piping bag fitted with a large round tip. Pipe small mounds onto the prepared baking sheet, leaving space between each puff.

Bake:
- Bake in the preheated oven for 15 minutes, then reduce the temperature to 375°F (190°C) and continue baking for an additional 15-20 minutes or until the cream puffs are golden brown and puffed.

Cool:
- Allow the cream puffs to cool completely on a wire rack.

Making the Whipped Cream Filling:

Whip Cream:
- In a large bowl, whip the heavy cream, powdered sugar, and vanilla extract until stiff peaks form.

Fill Puffs:
- Cut the cooled cream puffs in half horizontally. Fill the bottom halves with the whipped cream using a spoon or piping bag.

Top with Lids:
- Place the top halves back on the cream puffs.

Making the Chocolate Ganache (Optional):

Melt Chocolate:
- In a heatproof bowl, melt the chopped dark chocolate with heavy cream over a double boiler or in the microwave, stirring until smooth.

Add Butter:
- Stir in butter until fully melted.

Dip Puffs:
- Dip the top of each cream puff into the chocolate ganache, allowing any excess to drip off.

Chill:
- Place the chocolate-dipped cream puffs in the refrigerator for the chocolate to set.

Serve and Enjoy:
- Once the chocolate ganache has set, your cream puffs are ready to be served. Enjoy these delightful, airy pastries!

These cream puffs are a perfect combination of light choux pastry and creamy whipped cream filling. Feel free to get creative with different fillings or toppings to suit your preferences.

Profiteroles

Ingredients:

For the Choux Pastry:

- 1/2 cup (1 stick or 113g) unsalted butter
- 1 cup (240ml) water
- 1 cup (125g) all-purpose flour
- 1/4 teaspoon salt
- 4 large eggs

For the Whipped Cream Filling:

- 2 cups (480ml) heavy cream
- 1/2 cup (60g) powdered sugar
- 1 teaspoon vanilla extract

For the Chocolate Sauce:

- 4 ounces (120g) dark chocolate, chopped
- 1/2 cup (120ml) heavy cream
- 2 tablespoons (30g) unsalted butter
- 2 tablespoons (30g) powdered sugar (optional, for additional sweetness)

Instructions:

Making the Choux Pastry:

Preheat the Oven:
- Preheat your oven to 425°F (220°C). Line a baking sheet with parchment paper.

Prepare the Dough:
- In a saucepan, combine butter, water, and salt. Bring to a boil. Remove from heat and add flour all at once. Stir vigorously until the mixture forms a ball.

Add Eggs:
- Add eggs one at a time, beating well after each addition. The dough should be smooth and glossy.

Pipe Profiteroles:
- Transfer the choux pastry dough to a piping bag fitted with a large round tip. Pipe small mounds onto the prepared baking sheet, leaving space between each profiterole.

Bake:

- Bake in the preheated oven for 15 minutes, then reduce the temperature to 375°F (190°C) and continue baking for an additional 15-20 minutes or until the profiteroles are golden brown and puffed.

Cool:
- Allow the profiteroles to cool completely on a wire rack.

Making the Whipped Cream Filling:

Whip Cream:
- In a large bowl, whip the heavy cream, powdered sugar, and vanilla extract until stiff peaks form.

Fill Profiteroles:
- Cut the cooled profiteroles in half horizontally. Fill the bottom halves with the whipped cream using a spoon or piping bag.

Top with Lids:
- Place the top halves back on the profiteroles.

Making the Chocolate Sauce:

Melt Chocolate:
- In a heatproof bowl, melt the chopped dark chocolate with heavy cream over a double boiler or in the microwave, stirring until smooth.

Add Butter:
- Stir in butter until fully melted. Optionally, whisk in powdered sugar for additional sweetness.

Dip Profiteroles:
- Dip the top of each profiterole into the chocolate sauce, allowing any excess to drip off.

Chill:
- Place the chocolate-dipped profiteroles in the refrigerator for the chocolate to set.

Serve and Enjoy:
- Once the chocolate sauce has set, your profiteroles are ready to be served. Enjoy these delightful cream-filled pastries!

These profiteroles are a delightful treat with a perfect balance of light choux pastry, creamy filling, and rich chocolate sauce. They make an elegant and delicious dessert for special occasions.

Napoleons (Mille-Feuille)

Ingredients:

For the Puff Pastry:

- 1 sheet of puff pastry, thawed if frozen

For the Pastry Cream:

- 2 cups (480ml) whole milk
- 1/2 cup (100g) granulated sugar
- 1/4 cup (30g) cornstarch
- 4 large egg yolks
- 2 tablespoons (30g) unsalted butter
- 1 teaspoon vanilla extract

For Assembly:

- Confectioners' sugar for dusting (optional)

Instructions:

Making the Puff Pastry:

Preheat the Oven:
- Preheat your oven according to the puff pastry package instructions.

Roll Out Puff Pastry:
- On a lightly floured surface, roll out the puff pastry to a rectangle. Prick the surface with a fork to prevent excessive puffing.

Bake:
- Bake the puff pastry in the preheated oven according to the package instructions or until it's golden brown and puffed. Allow it to cool completely.

Making the Pastry Cream:

Heat Milk:
- In a saucepan, heat the whole milk until it just begins to simmer. Do not let it boil.

Whisk Sugar and Egg Yolks:
- In a separate bowl, whisk together the granulated sugar, cornstarch, and egg yolks until well combined.

Temper Eggs:

- Gradually pour a small amount of the hot milk into the egg mixture, whisking constantly to temper the eggs.

Cook Custard:
- Pour the tempered egg mixture back into the saucepan with the remaining milk. Cook over medium heat, stirring constantly, until the mixture thickens into a custard.

Add Butter and Vanilla:
- Remove from heat and stir in the butter and vanilla extract until the butter is melted and the vanilla is incorporated.

Cool:
- Allow the pastry cream to cool to room temperature. You can place a piece of plastic wrap directly on the surface to prevent a skin from forming.

Assembling the Napoleons:

Cut Puff Pastry:
- Once the puff pastry has cooled, cut it into equal-sized rectangles.

Layering:
- Place one rectangle of puff pastry on a serving plate. Spoon a layer of pastry cream over it. Repeat the process, layering puff pastry and pastry cream until you have the desired number of layers.

Top with Puff Pastry:
- Place a final layer of puff pastry on top. Optionally, dust with confectioners' sugar for a decorative touch.

Chill:
- Refrigerate the Napoleons for at least an hour to allow the layers to set.

Slice and Serve:
- Use a sharp knife to slice the Napoleons into individual portions. Serve chilled and enjoy!

These Napoleons are a delightful combination of flaky puff pastry and creamy pastry cream. They make an elegant and delicious dessert for special occasions or whenever you crave a taste of French pastry perfection.

Turnovers (Fruit or Savory)

Ingredients:

For the Dough:

- 2 sheets of puff pastry, thawed if frozen

For the Fruit Filling (Sweet Option):

- 2 cups diced fruits (e.g., apples, berries, peaches)
- 1/4 cup granulated sugar
- 1 tablespoon cornstarch
- 1 teaspoon lemon juice
- 1/2 teaspoon ground cinnamon (optional)

For the Savory Filling:

- 1 cup cooked and diced meat (e.g., chicken, ham, turkey)
- 1/2 cup diced vegetables (e.g., bell peppers, onions, spinach)
- 1/2 cup shredded cheese (optional)
- Salt and pepper to taste
- Herbs or spices of your choice (e.g., thyme, rosemary, paprika)

Additional for Both:

- 1 egg (for egg wash)
- Powdered sugar for dusting (for sweet turnovers, optional)

Instructions:

Making the Turnovers:

Preheat the Oven:
- Preheat your oven according to the puff pastry package instructions.

Prepare the Filling:
- For sweet turnovers, mix the diced fruits with sugar, cornstarch, lemon juice, and cinnamon in a bowl. For savory turnovers, combine cooked meat, diced vegetables, cheese, and seasonings in a bowl.

Roll Out Puff Pastry:
- On a lightly floured surface, roll out the puff pastry sheets to smooth out any creases.

Cut into Squares:

- Cut each puff pastry sheet into squares of your desired size.

Fill and Seal:
- Place a spoonful of filling in the center of each square. Fold the pastry over the filling to form a triangle or rectangle. Use a fork to press and seal the edges.

Egg Wash:
- Beat the egg and brush it over the top of each turnover. This gives the turnovers a golden, shiny finish.

Bake:
- Place the turnovers on a baking sheet lined with parchment paper. Bake in the preheated oven for about 15-20 minutes or until they are golden brown and puffed.

Cool:
- Allow the turnovers to cool on a wire rack.

Dust or Glaze (Optional):
- For sweet turnovers, you can dust them with powdered sugar. For a glaze, you can mix powdered sugar with a little milk or water and drizzle it over the turnovers.

Serve and Enjoy:
- Once cooled, your turnovers are ready to be served. Enjoy these delightful treats with your favorite fillings!

Feel free to get creative with the fillings and experiment with different combinations of fruits, meats, and vegetables. Turnovers are a versatile and delicious pastry that can be enjoyed for breakfast, dessert, or as a savory snack.

Fruit-Filled Pastries:

Apple Strudel

Ingredients:

For the Dough:

- 2 cups all-purpose flour
- 1/2 cup warm water
- 1/4 cup vegetable oil
- 1 egg
- 1/2 teaspoon salt
- 1 tablespoon white vinegar

For the Filling:

- 4-5 medium-sized apples (e.g., Granny Smith or Honeycrisp), peeled, cored, and thinly sliced
- 1/2 cup granulated sugar
- 1/2 cup breadcrumbs
- 1/2 cup raisins
- 1/2 cup chopped walnuts or almonds (optional)
- 1 teaspoon ground cinnamon
- Zest of 1 lemon
- Juice of 1/2 lemon

For Assembly:

- 1/2 cup melted unsalted butter
- Powdered sugar for dusting

Instructions:

Making the Dough:

    Prepare Dough:
- In a large bowl, combine flour, warm water, vegetable oil, egg, salt, and vinegar. Mix until a dough forms.

    Knead Dough:
- Knead the dough on a floured surface until smooth and elastic. Form it into a ball, coat with oil, and let it rest in a covered bowl for about 1 hour.

Roll Out Dough:
- Roll out the dough on a floured surface into a large, thin rectangle. You should be able to see your hand through it.

Making the Filling:

Preheat Oven:
- Preheat your oven to 375°F (190°C).

Prepare Filling:
- In a large bowl, mix sliced apples, granulated sugar, breadcrumbs, raisins, nuts (if using), ground cinnamon, lemon zest, and lemon juice.

Assembling the Strudel:

Layer with Butter:
- Brush the rolled-out dough with melted butter, leaving a border around the edges.

Add Filling:
- Spread the apple filling evenly over the buttered area.

Roll Up:
- Using the help of a kitchen towel, roll up the strudel tightly from the longer side, creating a log shape.

Place on Baking Sheet:
- Transfer the rolled strudel onto a parchment-lined baking sheet, with the seam side facing down.

Brush with Butter:
- Brush the top of the strudel with additional melted butter.

Bake:
- Bake in the preheated oven for about 35-40 minutes or until the strudel is golden brown and crispy.

Cool:
- Allow the strudel to cool for a bit before slicing.

Dust with Powdered Sugar:
- Dust the cooled apple strudel with powdered sugar before serving.

Serve and Enjoy:
- Slice the apple strudel into portions and serve warm. It can be enjoyed on its own or with a scoop of vanilla ice cream.

Apple strudel is a delightful dessert with layers of crisp, flaky dough and a sweet, spiced apple filling. It's perfect for any occasion and captures the comforting flavors of fall.

Mixed Berry Tart

Ingredients:

For the Tart Crust:

- 1 and 1/4 cups all-purpose flour
- 1/2 cup unsalted butter, chilled and cubed
- 1/4 cup granulated sugar
- 1/4 teaspoon salt
- 1 large egg yolk
- 2 tablespoons ice water

For the Berry Filling:

- 3 cups mixed berries (strawberries, blueberries, raspberries, blackberries)
- 1/2 cup granulated sugar (adjust according to the sweetness of the berries)
- 2 tablespoons cornstarch
- 1 tablespoon lemon juice

For the Glaze (Optional):

- 1/4 cup apricot preserves or berry jam
- 1 tablespoon water

Instructions:

Making the Tart Crust:

Preheat Oven:
- Preheat your oven to 375°F (190°C).

Prepare Tart Crust:
- In a food processor, combine flour, cold butter, sugar, and salt. Pulse until the mixture resembles coarse crumbs.

Add Egg Yolk:
- Add the egg yolk and pulse again. With the processor running, gradually add ice water until the dough comes together.

Form Dough:
- Turn the dough out onto a floured surface and form it into a disk. Wrap in plastic wrap and refrigerate for at least 30 minutes.

Roll Out Dough:

- On a floured surface, roll out the chilled dough to fit your tart pan. Press the dough into the pan, trimming any excess.

Prick with Fork:

- Prick the bottom of the tart crust with a fork. This prevents the crust from puffing up during baking.

Bake:

- Blind bake the tart crust by lining it with parchment paper and filling it with pie weights or dried beans. Bake for about 15 minutes. Remove the weights and bake for an additional 5-10 minutes or until golden brown. Allow it to cool completely.

Making the Berry Filling:

Prepare Berries:

- Wash and hull the strawberries. If using larger berries, cut them into bite-sized pieces.

Mix with Sugar and Cornstarch:

- In a bowl, gently toss the mixed berries with granulated sugar, cornstarch, and lemon juice until well coated.

Assembling the Tart:

Fill Tart Crust:

- Spoon the berry mixture into the cooled tart crust, spreading it evenly.

Bake:

- Bake the tart in the preheated oven for 25-30 minutes or until the berries are bubbly and the crust is golden brown.

Cool:

- Allow the tart to cool completely on a wire rack.

Optional Glaze:

Prepare Glaze:

- In a small saucepan, heat the apricot preserves or berry jam with water until melted and smooth.

Strain (Optional):

- If you prefer a smoother glaze, you can strain the mixture to remove fruit pieces.

Brush Tart:

- Brush the cooled tart with the glaze to give it a shiny finish.

Chill (Optional):

- Refrigerate the tart for a short time to set the glaze.

Serve and Enjoy:

- Slice the Mixed Berry Tart into wedges and serve. It's delicious on its own or with a dollop of whipped cream or a scoop of vanilla ice cream.

This Mixed Berry Tart is a beautiful and tasty dessert, perfect for showcasing the best of summer berries. Enjoy its sweet and tart flavors with a buttery, flaky crust!

Peach Galette

Ingredients:

For the Galette Dough:

- 1 and 1/4 cups all-purpose flour
- 1/2 cup unsalted butter, cold and cubed
- 2 tablespoons granulated sugar
- 1/4 teaspoon salt
- 3-4 tablespoons ice water

For the Peach Filling:

- 4-5 ripe peaches, sliced
- 1/3 cup granulated sugar
- 2 tablespoons cornstarch
- 1 teaspoon vanilla extract
- Zest of 1 lemon

For Assembly:

- 1 tablespoon unsalted butter, melted (for brushing)
- 1-2 tablespoons granulated sugar (for sprinkling)

Instructions:

Making the Galette Dough:

Combine Ingredients:
- In a food processor, pulse together flour, cold butter, sugar, and salt until the mixture resembles coarse crumbs.

Add Ice Water:
- With the processor running, gradually add ice water until the dough just comes together. Be careful not to overmix.

Form Dough:
- Turn the dough out onto a floured surface, gather it into a ball, flatten into a disk, wrap in plastic wrap, and refrigerate for at least 30 minutes.

Preparing the Peach Filling:

Slice Peaches:

- Peel and slice the ripe peaches. If they are very juicy, you can pat them with a paper towel to remove excess moisture.

Mix with Sugar and Cornstarch:
- In a bowl, gently toss the peach slices with granulated sugar, cornstarch, vanilla extract, and lemon zest. Set aside.

Assembling the Peach Galette:

Preheat Oven:
- Preheat your oven to 400°F (200°C).

Roll Out Dough:
- On a floured surface, roll out the chilled galette dough into a rough circle about 12 inches in diameter.

Transfer to Baking Sheet:
- Carefully transfer the rolled-out dough to a parchment-lined baking sheet.

Arrange Peach Slices:
- Arrange the sliced peaches in the center of the dough, leaving a border around the edges.

Fold Edges:
- Fold the edges of the dough over the peaches, pleating as you go, to create a rustic, free-form shape.

Brush with Butter:
- Brush the edges of the dough with melted butter.

Sprinkle with Sugar:
- Sprinkle the edges and the peaches with granulated sugar for a sweet, crispy finish.

Bake:
- Bake in the preheated oven for 30-35 minutes or until the crust is golden brown and the peaches are tender.

Cool:
- Allow the Peach Galette to cool slightly before slicing.

Serve and Enjoy:
- Serve the Peach Galette warm or at room temperature. It's delicious on its own or with a scoop of vanilla ice cream.

This Peach Galette is a simple and elegant dessert that captures the essence of ripe, juicy peaches. Enjoy its buttery crust and sweet peach filling, perfect for summer or any time you crave a delicious fruit pastry.

Blueberry Hand Pies

Ingredients:

For the Dough:

- 2 and 1/2 cups all-purpose flour
- 1 tablespoon granulated sugar
- 1/2 teaspoon salt
- 1 cup unsalted butter, cold and cubed
- 1/2 cup ice water

For the Blueberry Filling:

- 2 cups fresh or frozen blueberries
- 1/3 cup granulated sugar (adjust based on sweetness of blueberries)
- 1 tablespoon cornstarch
- 1 tablespoon lemon juice
- 1 teaspoon lemon zest

For Assembly:

- 1 egg (for egg wash)
- 1 tablespoon milk or water (for egg wash)
- Granulated sugar (for sprinkling)

Instructions:

Making the Dough:

> Combine Dry Ingredients:
> - In a bowl, whisk together flour, sugar, and salt.
>
> Cut in Butter:
> - Add cold, cubed butter to the flour mixture. Use a pastry cutter or your fingers to cut the butter into the flour until it resembles coarse crumbs.
>
> Add Ice Water:
> - Gradually add ice water to the dough, mixing just until the dough comes together. Form the dough into a ball, wrap it in plastic wrap, and refrigerate for at least 1 hour.

Preparing the Blueberry Filling:

Mix Ingredients:
- In a bowl, gently toss together blueberries, granulated sugar, cornstarch, lemon juice, and lemon zest until well combined.

Assembling the Blueberry Hand Pies:

Preheat Oven:
- Preheat your oven to 375°F (190°C).

Roll Out Dough:
- On a floured surface, roll out the chilled dough to about 1/8 inch thickness.

Cut Dough Circles:
- Use a round cookie cutter or a glass to cut out circles from the rolled-out dough. The size depends on your preference, but around 4-5 inches in diameter works well.

Add Blueberry Filling:
- Place a spoonful of the blueberry filling in the center of half of the dough circles, leaving a small border around the edges.

Top with Dough:
- Place another dough circle on top of each filled circle. Press the edges to seal.

Crimp Edges:
- Use a fork to crimp the edges of the hand pies, sealing them tightly.

Egg Wash:
- In a small bowl, beat the egg with milk or water to create an egg wash. Brush the tops of the hand pies with the egg wash.

Ventilation (Optional):
- Optionally, use a sharp knife to make a small slit or vents on the top of each hand pie to allow steam to escape during baking.

Sprinkle with Sugar:
- Sprinkle the tops of the hand pies with granulated sugar for a sweet, crispy finish.

Bake:
- Place the hand pies on a parchment-lined baking sheet and bake in the preheated oven for 20-25 minutes or until the crust is golden brown.

Cool:
- Allow the blueberry hand pies to cool slightly before serving.

Serve and Enjoy:
- Serve the hand pies warm or at room temperature. They're great on their own or with a scoop of vanilla ice cream.

These Blueberry Hand Pies are a delightful way to enjoy the sweetness of blueberries in a convenient and portable form. They make a perfect treat for picnics, parties, or simply satisfying your sweet tooth.

Cherry Almond Pastries

Ingredients:

For the Pastry:

- 1 sheet of puff pastry, thawed if frozen
- 1 cup cherries, pitted and halved
- 1/4 cup almond paste, crumbled
- 1 tablespoon granulated sugar
- 1 tablespoon all-purpose flour (for dusting)

For the Almond Glaze:

- 1/2 cup powdered sugar
- 1 tablespoon almond extract
- 1-2 tablespoons milk or water
- Sliced almonds for garnish (optional)

Instructions:

Preparing the Pastry:

Preheat Oven:
- Preheat your oven to 400°F (200°C).

Roll Out Puff Pastry:
- On a lightly floured surface, roll out the puff pastry into a rectangle.

Cut into Squares:
- Cut the rolled-out pastry into squares of your desired size.

Create an Almond Center:
- In the center of each pastry square, place a small amount of crumbled almond paste.

Add Cherries:
- Top the almond paste with halved cherries.

Fold and Seal:
- Fold the pastry squares over the cherries and almond paste, creating a triangle or rectangle shape. Press the edges to seal.

Dust with Sugar:
- Dust the tops of the pastries with granulated sugar for a sweet finish.

Bake:

- Place the pastries on a parchment-lined baking sheet and bake in the preheated oven for 15-20 minutes or until the pastry is golden brown and puffed.

Cool:
- Allow the Cherry Almond Pastries to cool on a wire rack.

Making the Almond Glaze:

Prepare Glaze:
- In a bowl, whisk together powdered sugar, almond extract, and enough milk or water to achieve a drizzling consistency.

Drizzle Glaze:
- Drizzle the almond glaze over the cooled pastries.

Garnish (Optional):
- Optionally, sprinkle sliced almonds on top of the glaze for added crunch and visual appeal.

Serve and Enjoy:
- Once the glaze has set, the Cherry Almond Pastries are ready to be served. Enjoy these delicious treats with a cup of tea or coffee.

These Cherry Almond Pastries are a delightful combination of flaky pastry, sweet cherries, and nutty almond flavor. They make for a lovely dessert or a special treat for brunch.

Raspberry Linzer Tarts

Ingredients:

For the Almond Pastry:

- 1 cup unsalted butter, softened
- 3/4 cup granulated sugar
- 1 large egg
- 1 teaspoon vanilla extract
- 2 cups all-purpose flour
- 1 cup ground almonds
- 1/2 teaspoon baking powder
- 1/4 teaspoon salt

For Assembly:

- Raspberry jam or preserves
- Confectioners' sugar (for dusting)

Instructions:

Making the Almond Pastry:

Cream Butter and Sugar:
- In a large bowl, cream together softened butter and granulated sugar until light and fluffy.

Add Egg and Vanilla:
- Beat in the egg and vanilla extract until well combined.

Combine Dry Ingredients:
- In a separate bowl, whisk together flour, ground almonds, baking powder, and salt.

Mix the Dough:
- Gradually add the dry ingredients to the wet ingredients, mixing until a soft dough forms.

Chill Dough:
- Divide the dough in half, form two discs, wrap them in plastic wrap, and refrigerate for at least 1 hour or until firm.

Assembling Raspberry Linzer Tarts:

Preheat Oven:

- Preheat your oven to 350°F (180°C).

Roll Out Dough:
- On a floured surface, roll out one disc of the chilled dough to about 1/8 inch thickness.

Cut Out Shapes:
- Using a round cookie cutter or a glass, cut out circles for the base of the tarts. For half of the circles, use a smaller round cutter to create a window in the center.

Transfer to Baking Sheet:
- Place the larger circles on a parchment-lined baking sheet, leaving space between them.

Bake Base:
- Bake the larger circles in the preheated oven for about 10-12 minutes or until the edges are lightly golden. These will be the bases of the tarts.

Roll Out Top Dough:
- Roll out the second disc of dough and cut out circles for the tops. These will have a window in the center.

Bake Tops:
- Bake the smaller circles in the preheated oven for about 8-10 minutes or until lightly golden.

Assemble:
- Allow both the bases and tops to cool completely. Spread a layer of raspberry jam on each base, leaving the window clear.

Place Top with Window:
- Gently place the top with the window on each base to create a sandwich. The jam will be visible through the window.

Dust with Sugar:
- Dust the tops of the tarts with confectioners' sugar for a finishing touch.

Serve and Enjoy:
- Raspberry Linzer Tarts are ready to be served. Enjoy these delightful treats with a cup of tea or coffee.

These Raspberry Linzer Tarts are not only delicious but also visually appealing with their window design. They make for an elegant dessert for special occasions or as a sweet treat for afternoon tea.

Lemon Curd Tartlets

Ingredients:

For the Tartlet Shells:

- 1 and 1/4 cups all-purpose flour
- 1/2 cup unsalted butter, cold and cubed
- 1/4 cup granulated sugar
- 1 large egg yolk
- 2 tablespoons ice water

For the Lemon Curd:

- 3/4 cup fresh lemon juice (about 4-5 lemons)
- Zest of 2 lemons
- 1 cup granulated sugar
- 4 large eggs
- 1/2 cup unsalted butter, melted

For Garnish (Optional):

- Powdered sugar
- Fresh berries or mint leaves

Instructions:

Making the Tartlet Shells:

Preheat Oven:
- Preheat your oven to 350°F (180°C).

Prepare Tartlet Dough:
- In a food processor, combine flour, cold butter, and sugar. Pulse until the mixture resembles coarse crumbs.

Add Egg Yolk:
- Add the egg yolk and pulse again. With the processor running, gradually add ice water until the dough comes together.

Form Dough:
- Turn the dough out onto a floured surface and form it into a disk. Wrap in plastic wrap and refrigerate for at least 30 minutes.

Roll Out Dough:

- On a floured surface, roll out the chilled dough to about 1/8 inch thickness. Cut out circles to fit your mini tartlet pans.

Press into Pans:
- Press the dough circles into the mini tartlet pans, ensuring an even layer. Trim any excess.

Bake:
- Bake the tartlet shells in the preheated oven for 12-15 minutes or until golden brown. Allow them to cool completely.

Making the Lemon Curd:

Prepare Double Boiler:
- Set up a double boiler or a heatproof bowl over a pot of simmering water.

Whisk Ingredients:
- In the double boiler, whisk together lemon juice, lemon zest, sugar, and eggs until well combined.

Cook and Stir:
- Cook the mixture over medium heat, stirring constantly, until it thickens and coats the back of a spoon (about 10-12 minutes).

Add Melted Butter:
- Remove the lemon curd from heat and whisk in the melted butter until smooth.

Strain (Optional):
- If desired, strain the lemon curd through a fine-mesh sieve to remove any zest or coagulated bits.

Cool:
- Allow the lemon curd to cool to room temperature.

Assembling the Lemon Curd Tartlets:

Fill Tartlet Shells:
- Spoon the cooled lemon curd into the baked tartlet shells, filling them to the top.

Chill:
- Refrigerate the tartlets for at least 1-2 hours to allow the lemon curd to set.

Garnish (Optional):
- Before serving, dust the tops with powdered sugar and garnish with fresh berries or mint leaves if desired.

Serve and Enjoy:

- Lemon Curd Tartlets are ready to be enjoyed. They make for a refreshing and tangy dessert.

These Lemon Curd Tartlets are perfect for serving at gatherings, tea parties, or as a delightful treat anytime you crave a burst of citrusy flavor.

Plum Frangipane Tart

Ingredients:

For the Tart Crust:

- 1 and 1/4 cups all-purpose flour
- 1/2 cup unsalted butter, cold and cubed
- 1/4 cup granulated sugar
- 1 large egg yolk
- 2 tablespoons ice water

For the Frangipane Filling:

- 1 cup almond flour
- 1/2 cup granulated sugar
- 1/2 cup unsalted butter, softened
- 2 large eggs
- 1 teaspoon almond extract

For Assembly:

- 4-5 ripe plums, thinly sliced
- 2 tablespoons apricot jam (for glazing, optional)
- Sliced almonds (for garnish, optional)

Instructions:

Making the Tart Crust:

    Preheat Oven:
- Preheat your oven to 375°F (190°C).

    Prepare Tart Crust:
- In a food processor, combine flour, cold butter, and sugar. Pulse until the mixture resembles coarse crumbs.

    Add Egg Yolk:
- Add the egg yolk and pulse again. With the processor running, gradually add ice water until the dough comes together.

    Form Dough:
- Turn the dough out onto a floured surface and form it into a disk. Wrap in plastic wrap and refrigerate for at least 30 minutes.

Roll Out Dough:
- On a floured surface, roll out the chilled dough to fit your tart pan. Press the dough into the tart pan, trimming any excess.

Bake:
- Bake the tart crust in the preheated oven for 15-20 minutes or until lightly golden. Allow it to cool.

Making the Frangipane Filling:

Prepare Frangipane:
- In a bowl, cream together almond flour, sugar, softened butter, eggs, and almond extract until well combined.

Assembling the Plum Frangipane Tart:

Spread Frangipane:
- Spread the frangipane filling evenly over the cooled tart crust.

Arrange Plum Slices:
- Arrange the thinly sliced plums over the frangipane filling in a decorative pattern.

Bake Again:
- Bake the tart in the preheated oven for 25-30 minutes or until the frangipane is set and the plums are tender.

Glaze (Optional):
- If desired, heat apricot jam in a small saucepan and brush it over the top of the tart for a glossy finish.

Garnish (Optional):
- Optionally, sprinkle sliced almonds over the glazed tart for added texture.

Cool:
- Allow the Plum Frangipane Tart to cool before slicing.

Serve and Enjoy:
- Serve the tart slices at room temperature. It can be enjoyed on its own or with a dollop of whipped cream or a scoop of vanilla ice cream.

This Plum Frangipane Tart is a delightful combination of almond goodness and sweet, juicy plums. It's a beautiful and tasty dessert perfect for showcasing the seasonal bounty of plums.

Nut-Filled Pastries:

Baklava

Ingredients:

For the Filling:

- 1 cup almonds, finely chopped
- 1 cup walnuts, finely chopped
- 1 cup pistachios, finely chopped
- 1 cup sugar
- 1 tablespoon ground cinnamon

For the Phyllo Layers:

- 1 package (16 ounces) phyllo dough, thawed if frozen
- 1 cup unsalted butter, melted

For the Syrup:

- 1 cup water
- 1 cup granulated sugar
- 1/2 cup honey
- 1 cinnamon stick
- 1 teaspoon lemon juice

Instructions:

Preparing the Nut Filling:

> In a bowl, combine finely chopped almonds, walnuts, pistachios, sugar, and ground cinnamon. Set aside.

Assembling the Baklava:

> Preheat your oven to 350°F (175°C).
> Trim the phyllo dough sheets to fit the size of your baking dish. Cover the sheets with a damp kitchen towel to prevent drying out.
> Brush the bottom of a baking dish with melted butter.
> Place one sheet of phyllo dough in the dish and brush it with melted butter. Repeat, layering sheets and buttering each layer until you have about 8-10 sheets.
> Sprinkle a generous layer of the nut mixture over the phyllo layers.

Continue layering phyllo sheets and butter, followed by the nut mixture, until all the nuts are used. Finish with a top layer of phyllo sheets, ensuring to brush each one with butter. Using a sharp knife, cut the baklava into diamond or square shapes.

Bake in the preheated oven for 30-40 minutes or until golden brown and crisp.

Making the Syrup:

In a saucepan, combine water, sugar, honey, cinnamon stick, and lemon juice. Bring the mixture to a boil, then reduce the heat and let it simmer for about 10-15 minutes until it slightly thickens.

Remove the cinnamon stick and let the syrup cool.

Pouring the Syrup:

Once the baklava is out of the oven, immediately pour the cooled syrup evenly over the hot pastry.

Allow the baklava to cool and absorb the syrup for several hours or overnight before serving.

Serve the baklava at room temperature and enjoy!

Baklava is a sweet and nutty dessert with layers of flaky phyllo pastry drenched in a honey-sweetened syrup. It's a classic treat that's perfect for special occasions or as a delightful ending to a meal.

Almond Croissants

Ingredients:

For the Almond Cream:

- 1 cup almond flour
- 1/2 cup granulated sugar
- 1/2 cup unsalted butter, softened
- 2 large eggs
- 1 teaspoon almond extract
- 1/4 cup all-purpose flour

For the Croissants:

- Croissants (store-bought or homemade)
- 1/2 cup apricot jam (for glazing, optional)
- Sliced almonds (for topping)

Instructions:

Making the Almond Cream:

> In a bowl, combine almond flour, sugar, softened butter, eggs, almond extract, and all-purpose flour. Mix until you have a smooth almond cream. Set aside.

Assembling the Almond Croissants:

> Preheat your oven to 350°F (175°C).
> Slice each croissant horizontally, creating a top and bottom half.
> Spread a generous layer of almond cream on the bottom half of each croissant.
> Place the top half of the croissant back on and press gently to secure.
> Optionally, warm apricot jam in a saucepan and brush it over the tops of the assembled croissants for a glossy finish.
> Sprinkle sliced almonds on top of the almond cream.
> Place the almond-filled croissants on a baking sheet.
> Bake in the preheated oven for about 15-20 minutes or until the almond cream is set, and the croissants are golden brown.
> Remove from the oven and allow them to cool.
> Once cooled, dust with powdered sugar if desired.
> Serve and enjoy your delicious Almond Croissants!

These Almond Croissants are a delightful twist on the classic croissant, featuring a rich almond filling that adds a nutty and sweet flavor. They make for a perfect breakfast or a special treat for brunch.

Pecan Pie Bars

Ingredients:

For the Crust:

- 1 and 1/2 cups all-purpose flour
- 1/2 cup unsalted butter, softened
- 1/4 cup granulated sugar
- 1/4 teaspoon salt

For the Pecan Filling:

- 3/4 cup unsalted butter
- 1 cup packed brown sugar
- 1/2 cup honey or corn syrup
- 2 cups pecans, chopped
- 2 teaspoons vanilla extract
- 1/4 teaspoon salt

Instructions:

Making the Crust:

Preheat your oven to 350°F (175°C). Grease a 9x13-inch baking pan.
In a bowl, combine the softened butter, flour, sugar, and salt. Mix until the ingredients come together to form a crumbly dough.
Press the dough into the prepared baking pan, creating an even crust layer.
Bake the crust in the preheated oven for 15-20 minutes or until lightly golden.
Remove from the oven and set aside.

Making the Pecan Filling:

In a saucepan over medium heat, melt the butter.
Stir in the brown sugar and honey (or corn syrup) until the mixture is well combined and smooth.
Remove the saucepan from heat and stir in the chopped pecans, vanilla extract, and salt.

Assembling and Baking:

Pour the pecan filling evenly over the pre-baked crust.

Return the pan to the oven and bake for an additional 20-25 minutes or until the filling is set.
Remove from the oven and let the Pecan Pie Bars cool completely in the pan.
Once cooled, cut into squares or bars.
Serve and enjoy your delicious Pecan Pie Bars!

These bars are a wonderful alternative to traditional pecan pie, offering the same delightful flavors in a convenient and shareable form. They make for a fantastic dessert for holidays, potlucks, or any occasion where you want to treat yourself and others to a sweet indulgence.

Hazelnut Pinwheels

Ingredients:

For the Dough:

- 2 and 1/4 cups all-purpose flour
- 1 cup unsalted butter, cold and cubed
- 1/2 cup granulated sugar
- 1/4 teaspoon salt
- 1/2 cup sour cream
- 1 teaspoon vanilla extract

For the Hazelnut Filling:

- 1 cup hazelnuts, toasted and finely chopped
- 1/2 cup granulated sugar
- 2 tablespoons unsalted butter, melted
- 1 teaspoon ground cinnamon

For Assembly:

- 1 egg (for egg wash)
- Powdered sugar (for dusting, optional)

Instructions:

Making the Dough:

> In a food processor, combine the flour, cold cubed butter, sugar, and salt. Pulse until the mixture resembles coarse crumbs.
> Add the sour cream and vanilla extract. Pulse again until the dough comes together. Do not overmix.
> Turn the dough out onto a floured surface and knead it briefly to form a smooth ball. Divide the dough in half, shape each half into a disk, wrap in plastic wrap, and refrigerate for at least 1 hour.

Making the Hazelnut Filling:

> In a bowl, mix together the finely chopped toasted hazelnuts, sugar, melted butter, and ground cinnamon to create the hazelnut filling. Set aside.

Assembling the Hazelnut Pinwheels:

Preheat your oven to 350°F (175°C). Line baking sheets with parchment paper.
Take one disk of the chilled dough and roll it out on a floured surface into a rectangle, approximately 12x8 inches.
Spread half of the hazelnut filling evenly over the rolled-out dough.
Starting from the longer side, carefully roll the dough into a log or cylinder.
Repeat the process with the second disk of dough and the remaining hazelnut filling.
Place the rolled logs in the refrigerator for about 15-20 minutes to firm up.
Remove the logs from the refrigerator and slice them into rounds, approximately 1/2 inch thick.
Place the pinwheel slices on the prepared baking sheets, leaving some space between each.
In a small bowl, beat the egg to create an egg wash. Brush the tops of the pinwheels with the egg wash.
Bake in the preheated oven for 12-15 minutes or until the edges are golden brown.
Allow the Hazelnut Pinwheels to cool on the baking sheets for a few minutes before transferring them to a wire rack to cool completely.
Optionally, dust the cooled pinwheels with powdered sugar.
Serve and enjoy your Hazelnut Pinwheels as a delightful pastry treat.

These Hazelnut Pinwheels are a perfect blend of flaky pastry and sweet, nutty filling, making them a delightful addition to your dessert repertoire or a special treat for afternoon tea.

Walnut Rugelach

Ingredients:

For the Dough:

- 1 cup unsalted butter, softened
- 8 ounces cream cheese, softened
- 2 cups all-purpose flour
- 1/4 cup granulated sugar
- 1/4 teaspoon salt
- 1 teaspoon vanilla extract

For the Walnut Filling:

- 1 cup walnuts, finely chopped
- 1/2 cup granulated sugar
- 1 teaspoon ground cinnamon
- 1/4 cup apricot preserves or jam

For Assembly:

- Powdered sugar (for dusting, optional)

Instructions:

Making the Dough:

In a large bowl, cream together the softened butter and cream cheese until smooth. Add the flour, sugar, salt, and vanilla extract. Mix until the dough comes together. Divide the dough into 4 equal portions, shape each into a disk, wrap in plastic wrap, and refrigerate for at least 1 hour.

Making the Walnut Filling:

In a bowl, mix together the finely chopped walnuts, sugar, and ground cinnamon to create the walnut filling.
Preheat your oven to 350°F (175°C). Line baking sheets with parchment paper.

Assembling the Walnut Rugelach:

Take one disk of the chilled dough and roll it out on a floured surface into a circle, approximately 1/8 inch thick.
Spread a thin layer of apricot preserves or jam over the rolled-out dough.

Sprinkle a quarter of the walnut filling evenly over the jam-covered dough.

Using a pizza cutter or a sharp knife, cut the dough into 8 wedges.

Starting from the wider end, roll each wedge into a crescent shape.

Place the rolled rugelach on the prepared baking sheets, with the pointed end underneath.

Repeat the process with the remaining dough and filling.

Bake in the preheated oven for 15-18 minutes or until the rugelach are golden brown.

Allow the Walnut Rugelach to cool on the baking sheets for a few minutes before transferring them to a wire rack to cool completely.

Optionally, dust the cooled rugelach with powdered sugar.

Serve and enjoy your Walnut Rugelach as a delightful and nutty pastry treat.

These Walnut Rugelach are perfect for holiday celebrations, afternoon tea, or as a sweet indulgence anytime. The combination of flaky dough and a sweet walnut filling makes them a crowd-pleaser.

Chocolate-Lovers' Pastries:

Chocolate Babka

Ingredients:

For the Dough:

- 4 to 4.5 cups all-purpose flour
- 1/2 cup granulated sugar
- 1 tablespoon active dry yeast
- 1 cup whole milk, warmed to about 110°F (43°C)
- 1/2 cup unsalted butter, softened
- 2 large eggs
- 1 teaspoon vanilla extract
- 1/2 teaspoon salt

For the Chocolate Filling:

- 1 cup chocolate chips or finely chopped chocolate
- 1/2 cup unsalted butter
- 1/2 cup powdered sugar
- 1/4 cup cocoa powder
- 1 teaspoon ground cinnamon

For the Syrup (Optional):

- 1/2 cup water
- 1/2 cup granulated sugar

Instructions:

Making the Dough:

> In a small bowl, combine warm milk and 1 tablespoon of sugar. Sprinkle the yeast over the mixture, stir gently, and let it sit for about 5-10 minutes until foamy.
> In a large bowl or stand mixer, combine the softened butter and sugar. Mix until creamy.
> Add the eggs, vanilla extract, and the yeast mixture. Mix well.
> Gradually add the flour and salt, mixing until a soft dough forms.
> Knead the dough on a floured surface or in the mixer with a dough hook for about 5-7 minutes until it becomes smooth and elastic.

Place the dough in a greased bowl, cover with a damp cloth, and let it rise in a warm place for about 1-2 hours or until it doubles in size.

Making the Chocolate Filling:

In a saucepan over low heat, melt the butter. Add the chocolate, powdered sugar, cocoa powder, and ground cinnamon. Stir until the chocolate is completely melted and the mixture is smooth. Remove from heat and let it cool slightly.

Assembling the Chocolate Babka:

Preheat your oven to 350°F (175°C). Grease and flour two loaf pans.
Divide the risen dough into two equal parts.
Roll out each portion into a rectangle on a floured surface.
Spread half of the chocolate filling over each rectangle, leaving a small border around the edges.
Roll each rectangle tightly into a log.
Using a sharp knife, cut each log in half lengthwise to expose the layers of chocolate.
Twist the two halves together, creating a braided effect.
Place the twisted dough into the prepared loaf pans.
Let the babkas rise for another 30 minutes.
Bake in the preheated oven for 25-30 minutes or until golden brown.

Making the Syrup (Optional):

In a small saucepan, combine water and sugar. Bring to a boil, then reduce heat and simmer for a few minutes until the sugar dissolves.
Brush the warm syrup over the baked babkas to add a shiny finish.

Serving:

Allow the Chocolate Babka to cool in the pans for a few minutes before transferring them to a wire rack to cool completely.
Slice and enjoy!

Chocolate Babka is a delightful treat with a soft and rich bread texture complemented by layers of sweet chocolate. It's perfect for breakfast, brunch, or as a sweet indulgence with your favorite hot beverage.

Chocolate Éclairs

Ingredients:

For the Choux Pastry:

- 1 cup water
- 1/2 cup unsalted butter
- 1 cup all-purpose flour
- 4 large eggs

For the Pastry Cream Filling:

- 2 cups whole milk
- 1/2 cup granulated sugar
- 1/4 cup cornstarch
- 4 large egg yolks
- 2 teaspoons vanilla extract

For the Chocolate Icing:

- 1 cup semisweet chocolate chips or chopped chocolate
- 1/2 cup heavy cream
- 2 tablespoons unsalted butter
- 1 cup powdered sugar (optional, for a sweeter icing)

Instructions:

Making the Choux Pastry:

    Preheat your oven to 425°F (220°C). Line a baking sheet with parchment paper. In a medium saucepan, combine water and butter over medium heat. Bring to a boil.
    Add the flour all at once and stir vigorously with a wooden spoon until the mixture forms a ball and pulls away from the sides of the pan.
    Remove from heat and let it cool for a couple of minutes.
    Add eggs one at a time, beating well after each addition, until the dough is smooth and glossy.
    Transfer the choux pastry to a piping bag fitted with a large round tip.
    Pipe the dough onto the prepared baking sheet into 4 to 6-inch long logs, leaving space between each éclair.

Bake in the preheated oven for 15 minutes, then reduce the temperature to 375°F (190°C) and bake for an additional 10-15 minutes or until golden brown and puffed.

Allow the éclairs to cool completely before filling.

Making the Pastry Cream Filling:

In a saucepan, heat the milk until it just begins to simmer.
In a bowl, whisk together sugar, cornstarch, and egg yolks until well combined.
Slowly pour the hot milk into the egg mixture, whisking constantly.
Return the mixture to the saucepan and cook over medium heat, stirring constantly, until it thickens.
Remove from heat, stir in vanilla extract, and let the pastry cream cool.

Filling the Éclairs:

Once the éclairs are cooled, use a sharp knife to make a small slit along the side.
Fill a piping bag fitted with a small round tip with the cooled pastry cream.
Pipe the pastry cream into the éclairs through the slit.

Making the Chocolate Icing:

In a heatproof bowl, combine chocolate, heavy cream, and butter.
Melt the mixture over a double boiler or in the microwave, stirring until smooth.
If you prefer a sweeter icing, whisk in powdered sugar until well combined.
Dip the tops of the filled éclairs into the chocolate icing or spoon the icing over the éclairs.
Allow the chocolate icing to set before serving.

Chocolate éclairs are now ready to be enjoyed! These delightful pastries are perfect for special occasions, dessert tables, or as an elegant treat for any time you crave a delicious combination of creamy filling and chocolatey goodness.

Chocolate Croissants

Ingredients:

For the Dough:

- 2 and 1/4 teaspoons (1 packet) active dry yeast
- 1/4 cup warm water (about 110°F or 43°C)
- 1/2 cup cold milk
- 1/4 cup granulated sugar
- 2 cups all-purpose flour, plus more for dusting
- 1/2 teaspoon salt
- 1 cup unsalted butter, cold

For the Chocolate Filling:

- 4 ounces (about 1/2 cup) good quality dark chocolate, chopped or chocolate chips
- 2 tablespoons unsalted butter

For Assembly:

- 1 egg (for egg wash)
- Powdered sugar (optional, for dusting)

Instructions:

Making the Dough:

> In a small bowl, dissolve the yeast in warm water and let it sit for about 5 minutes until it becomes frothy.
> In a separate bowl, combine cold milk and granulated sugar.
> In a large bowl or stand mixer, mix together the flour and salt. Add the frothy yeast mixture and the milk-sugar mixture. Mix until a dough forms.
> Turn the dough out onto a floured surface and shape it into a rectangle. Wrap it in plastic wrap and refrigerate for at least 1 hour.
> While the dough is chilling, flatten the cold butter into a rectangle between sheets of parchment paper. Place it back in the refrigerator to keep it cold.
> Roll out the chilled dough on a floured surface into a larger rectangle.
> Place the cold butter rectangle on one half of the dough, then fold the other half over the butter. Seal the edges.

Roll out the dough-butter combination into a rectangle again and fold it into thirds, like a letter.

Repeat the rolling and folding process 2-3 more times, chilling the dough in the refrigerator between each fold.

After the final fold, wrap the dough in plastic wrap and refrigerate for at least 1 hour or overnight.

Filling and Shaping:

Preheat your oven to 400°F (200°C). Line a baking sheet with parchment paper.

Roll out the chilled dough on a floured surface into a large rectangle.

Melt the chocolate and butter together, then spread the mixture evenly over the dough.

Fold the dough in half lengthwise, covering the chocolate filling.

Cut the dough into triangles, then place a piece of chocolate at the wide end of each triangle.

Roll each triangle from the wide end towards the point, shaping it into a crescent.

Place the shaped chocolate croissants on the prepared baking sheet.

Baking:

Beat an egg and brush it over the tops of the croissants for a golden finish.

Bake in the preheated oven for 15-18 minutes or until the croissants are golden brown and puffed.

Remove from the oven and let them cool on a wire rack.

Optionally, dust the cooled chocolate croissants with powdered sugar before serving.

Enjoy your homemade chocolate croissants with a cup of coffee or tea. These flaky pastries with a rich chocolate filling are a delightful treat for breakfast or as an indulgent snack.

Chocolate Raspberry Tart

Ingredients:

For the Chocolate Tart Crust:

- 1 and 1/4 cups all-purpose flour
- 1/4 cup unsweetened cocoa powder
- 1/2 cup confectioners' sugar
- 1/4 teaspoon salt
- 1/2 cup unsalted butter, cold and cut into small pieces
- 1 large egg yolk
- 2 tablespoons ice water

For the Chocolate Ganache Filling:

- 8 ounces dark chocolate, finely chopped
- 1 cup heavy cream
- 2 tablespoons unsalted butter

For Topping:

- Fresh raspberries

Instructions:

Making the Chocolate Tart Crust:

>In a food processor, combine the flour, cocoa powder, confectioners' sugar, and salt. Pulse to mix.
>Add the cold, diced butter to the processor and pulse until the mixture resembles coarse crumbs.
>In a small bowl, whisk together the egg yolk and ice water.
>With the food processor running, gradually add the egg yolk mixture until the dough comes together.
>Turn the dough out onto a lightly floured surface and knead it a few times to bring it together.
>Flatten the dough into a disk, wrap it in plastic wrap, and refrigerate for at least 30 minutes.
>Preheat your oven to 375°F (190°C).

On a floured surface, roll out the chilled dough to fit your tart pan. Press the dough into the pan, trimming any excess.

Prick the bottom of the crust with a fork, line it with parchment paper, and fill it with pie weights or dried beans.

Bake in the preheated oven for about 15 minutes. Remove the parchment paper and weights, then bake for an additional 10 minutes or until the crust is set.

Allow the crust to cool completely.

Making the Chocolate Ganache Filling:

Place the finely chopped dark chocolate in a heatproof bowl.

In a small saucepan, heat the heavy cream until it just begins to simmer.

Pour the hot cream over the chopped chocolate and let it sit for a minute.

Stir the chocolate and cream together until smooth and well combined.

Add the butter and continue stirring until the ganache is glossy and the butter is fully melted.

Let the ganache cool slightly.

Assembling the Tart:

Pour the chocolate ganache into the cooled tart crust.

Refrigerate the tart for at least 2 hours or until the ganache is set.

Before serving, arrange fresh raspberries on top of the set chocolate ganache.

Optionally, dust the tart with a sprinkle of cocoa powder or confectioners' sugar.

Slice and serve your delicious Chocolate Raspberry Tart.

This Chocolate Raspberry Tart is a perfect blend of velvety chocolate and the bright, fruity flavor of raspberries. It's an elegant dessert that's sure to impress your guests and satisfy your sweet cravings.

Chocolate Almond Braid

Ingredients:

For the Dough:

- 2 and 1/4 teaspoons (1 packet) active dry yeast
- 1/4 cup warm water (about 110°F or 43°C)
- 1/2 cup granulated sugar
- 1/2 cup unsalted butter, softened
- 3/4 cup whole milk, warmed
- 3 large eggs
- 4 to 4.5 cups all-purpose flour
- 1/2 teaspoon salt

For the Chocolate Almond Filling:

- 1 cup chocolate chips or chopped chocolate
- 1/2 cup almond flour
- 1/4 cup granulated sugar
- 2 tablespoons unsweetened cocoa powder
- 1/4 cup unsalted butter, melted

For Assembly:

- 1 egg (for egg wash)
- Sliced almonds (for topping)
- Powdered sugar (optional, for dusting)

Instructions:

Making the Dough:

> In a small bowl, dissolve the yeast in warm water and let it sit for about 5 minutes until it becomes frothy.
> In a large bowl or stand mixer, combine sugar, softened butter, warmed milk, and eggs. Mix well.
> Add the frothy yeast mixture to the wet ingredients and mix again.
> Gradually add the flour and salt, mixing until a soft dough forms.
> Knead the dough on a floured surface or in the mixer with a dough hook for about 5-7 minutes until it becomes smooth and elastic.

Place the dough in a greased bowl, cover with a damp cloth, and let it rise in a warm place for about 1-2 hours or until it doubles in size.

Making the Chocolate Almond Filling:

In a bowl, combine chocolate chips, almond flour, sugar, cocoa powder, and melted butter. Mix until well combined.

Assembling the Chocolate Almond Braid:

Preheat your oven to 375°F (190°C). Line a baking sheet with parchment paper.
Punch down the risen dough and turn it out onto a floured surface.
Roll out the dough into a large rectangle.
Spread the chocolate almond filling evenly over the rectangle, leaving a small border around the edges.
Starting from one long side, roll the dough into a log.
Place the log onto the prepared baking sheet.
Using a sharp knife, cut the log in half lengthwise, leaving one end uncut.
Twist the two halves together, creating a braided effect. Seal the ends.
Beat an egg and brush it over the top of the braided dough.
Sprinkle sliced almonds over the top.

Baking:

Bake in the preheated oven for 25-30 minutes or until the braid is golden brown and sounds hollow when tapped.
Optional: Dust the cooled Chocolate Almond Braid with powdered sugar before serving.
Slice and enjoy your Chocolate Almond Braid!

This Chocolate Almond Braid is a beautiful and delicious treat, perfect for breakfast or brunch.

The combination of chocolate, almonds, and the soft, flaky pastry makes it an irresistible delight for any occasion.

Custard and Cream Pastries:

Vanilla Custard Tarts

Ingredients:

For the Tart Crust:

- 1 and 1/4 cups all-purpose flour
- 1/2 cup unsalted butter, cold and cut into small pieces
- 1/4 cup granulated sugar
- 1 large egg yolk
- 2 tablespoons ice water

For the Vanilla Custard Filling:

- 2 cups whole milk
- 1/2 cup granulated sugar
- 1/4 cup cornstarch
- 4 large egg yolks
- 2 teaspoons vanilla extract

Instructions:

Making the Tart Crust:

> In a food processor, combine the flour, cold butter, and sugar. Pulse until the mixture resembles coarse crumbs.
> Add the egg yolk and ice water, and pulse until the dough comes together.
> Turn the dough out onto a floured surface and knead it a few times to form a smooth ball.
> Flatten the dough into a disk, wrap it in plastic wrap, and refrigerate for at least 30 minutes.
> Preheat your oven to 375°F (190°C).
> On a floured surface, roll out the chilled dough and press it into individual tart pans.
> Prick the bottom of the crusts with a fork and bake in the preheated oven for about 12-15 minutes or until lightly golden. Allow the crusts to cool.

Making the Vanilla Custard Filling:

> In a saucepan, heat the whole milk over medium heat until it just begins to simmer.
> In a bowl, whisk together sugar, cornstarch, and egg yolks until well combined.

Slowly pour the hot milk into the egg mixture, whisking constantly.

Return the mixture to the saucepan and cook over medium heat, stirring constantly, until it thickens.

Remove from heat, stir in vanilla extract, and let the custard cool.

Assembling the Vanilla Custard Tarts:

Once the tart crusts and custard are both cooled, spoon the custard into the tart shells.

Smooth the surface of the custard with a spatula or spoon.

Optionally, refrigerate the tarts for an hour or more to allow the custard to set further.

Serve the Vanilla Custard Tarts at room temperature or chilled.

These Vanilla Custard Tarts are elegant and delicious, making them a perfect dessert for any occasion. The combination of the buttery tart crust and the silky vanilla custard filling creates a delightful treat that will be enjoyed by everyone.

Chocolate Mousse Tart

Ingredients:

For the Chocolate Tart Crust:

- 1 and 1/4 cups all-purpose flour
- 1/4 cup unsweetened cocoa powder
- 1/2 cup confectioners' sugar
- 1/4 teaspoon salt
- 1/2 cup unsalted butter, cold and cut into small pieces
- 1 large egg yolk
- 2 tablespoons ice water

For the Chocolate Mousse Filling:

- 8 ounces dark chocolate, finely chopped
- 1 cup heavy cream
- 1/4 cup confectioners' sugar
- 1 teaspoon vanilla extract

Optional Toppings:

- Whipped cream
- Chocolate shavings or grated chocolate

Instructions:

Making the Chocolate Tart Crust:

> In a food processor, combine the flour, cocoa powder, confectioners' sugar, and salt. Pulse to mix.
> Add the cold, diced butter to the processor and pulse until the mixture resembles coarse crumbs.
> In a small bowl, whisk together the egg yolk and ice water.
> With the food processor running, gradually add the egg yolk mixture until the dough comes together.
> Turn the dough out onto a lightly floured surface and knead it a few times to bring it together.
> Flatten the dough into a disk, wrap it in plastic wrap, and refrigerate for at least 30 minutes.

Preheat your oven to 375°F (190°C).

On a floured surface, roll out the chilled dough to fit your tart pan. Press the dough into the pan, trimming any excess.

Prick the bottom of the crust with a fork, line it with parchment paper, and fill it with pie weights or dried beans.

Bake in the preheated oven for about 15 minutes. Remove the parchment paper and weights, then bake for an additional 10 minutes or until the crust is set.

Allow the crust to cool completely.

Making the Chocolate Mousse Filling:

Place the finely chopped dark chocolate in a heatproof bowl.

In a small saucepan, heat the heavy cream until it just begins to simmer.

Pour the hot cream over the chopped chocolate and let it sit for a minute.

Stir the chocolate and cream together until smooth and well combined.

Add the confectioners' sugar and vanilla extract, and continue stirring until the mixture is glossy and smooth.

Allow the chocolate mousse to cool to room temperature.

Assembling the Tart:

Once the tart crust is cooled, pour the chocolate mousse filling into the tart shell.

Smooth the surface of the chocolate mousse with a spatula.

Refrigerate the Chocolate Mousse Tart for at least 2-3 hours or until the mousse is set.

Optional Toppings:

Before serving, you can add a dollop of whipped cream on top of the chocolate mousse.

Sprinkle chocolate shavings or grated chocolate for an extra touch.

Slice and serve your decadent Chocolate Mousse Tart.

This Chocolate Mousse Tart is a luscious and indulgent dessert that is sure to impress. The combination of the rich chocolate mousse and the cocoa-infused tart crust creates a delightful treat for chocolate lovers.

Creme Brulee

Ingredients:

- 2 cups heavy cream
- 1 vanilla bean or 1 teaspoon vanilla extract
- 5 large egg yolks
- 1/2 cup granulated sugar, plus extra for caramelizing

Instructions:

Preparing the Custard:

Preheat your oven to 325°F (160°C). Place ramekins in a baking dish.
In a saucepan, heat the heavy cream over medium heat until it's just about to simmer. If using a vanilla bean, split it lengthwise, scrape the seeds into the cream, and add the vanilla bean pod. If using vanilla extract, add it later.
In a separate bowl, whisk together the egg yolks and sugar until well combined.
Slowly pour the hot cream into the egg mixture, whisking continuously to avoid curdling.
If you used a vanilla bean, remove the pod from the mixture.
Pour the custard mixture into the ramekins.

Baking:

Create a water bath by pouring hot water into the baking dish around the ramekins until it reaches about halfway up the sides of the ramekins.
Bake in the preheated oven for approximately 40-45 minutes or until the custard is set but still slightly jiggly in the center.
Remove the ramekins from the water bath and let them cool to room temperature. Then, refrigerate them for at least 2-4 hours, or overnight.

Caramelizing the Sugar:

Prior to serving, sprinkle a thin, even layer of granulated sugar over the chilled custard.
Use a kitchen torch to caramelize the sugar by moving the flame in a circular motion until the sugar forms a golden-brown crust. Alternatively, you can place the ramekins under a broiler for a few minutes, but be sure to watch closely to prevent burning.
Allow the sugar to cool and harden before serving.

Serve and enjoy the delightful contrast between the creamy custard and the crisp, caramelized sugar topping.

Crème Brûlée is a sophisticated and timeless dessert that is sure to impress your guests with its silky texture and delightful flavor.

Banana Cream Pie

Ingredients:

For the Pie Crust:

- 1 and 1/4 cups all-purpose flour
- 1/2 cup unsalted butter, chilled and cut into small pieces
- 1/4 cup granulated sugar
- 1/4 teaspoon salt
- 3-4 tablespoons ice water

For the Filling:

- 3-4 ripe bananas, sliced
- 2 cups whole milk
- 3/4 cup granulated sugar
- 1/3 cup all-purpose flour
- 1/4 teaspoon salt
- 4 large egg yolks
- 2 teaspoons vanilla extract

For the Topping:

- 1 cup heavy cream
- 2 tablespoons powdered sugar
- 1 teaspoon vanilla extract

Instructions:

Making the Pie Crust:

> In a food processor, combine the flour, sugar, and salt. Pulse to mix.
> Add the chilled butter to the processor and pulse until the mixture resembles coarse crumbs.
> Gradually add the ice water, one tablespoon at a time, and pulse until the dough just comes together.
> Turn the dough out onto a floured surface, knead it a few times to form a smooth ball, and then flatten it into a disk.
> Wrap the dough in plastic wrap and refrigerate for at least 1 hour.
> Preheat your oven to 375°F (190°C).

On a floured surface, roll out the chilled dough to fit a 9-inch pie pan.
Press the dough into the pan, trim any excess, and crimp the edges.
Prick the bottom of the crust with a fork and bake in the preheated oven for about 15 minutes or until lightly golden. Allow the crust to cool completely.

Making the Filling:

In a saucepan, heat the whole milk until it's just about to simmer.
In a bowl, whisk together sugar, flour, and salt. Add the egg yolks and whisk until well combined.
Gradually pour the hot milk into the egg mixture, whisking constantly.
Return the mixture to the saucepan and cook over medium heat, stirring constantly, until it thickens.
Remove from heat, stir in vanilla extract, and let the custard cool to room temperature.

Assembling the Banana Cream Pie:

Place a layer of sliced bananas on the cooled pie crust.
Pour the cooled vanilla custard over the bananas, spreading it evenly.
Refrigerate the pie for at least 2-4 hours or until the custard is set.

Making the Whipped Cream Topping:

In a chilled bowl, whip the heavy cream until soft peaks form.
Add powdered sugar and vanilla extract, and continue whipping until stiff peaks form.

Topping the Pie:

Before serving, spread the whipped cream over the chilled banana custard.
Optionally, garnish with additional banana slices.
Slice and serve your delicious Banana Cream Pie.

This Banana Cream Pie is a delightful combination of buttery crust, creamy custard, and fresh bananas, topped with a light and fluffy whipped cream. It's a classic dessert that's perfect for any occasion.

Coconut Cream Pie

Ingredients:

For the Pie Crust:

- 1 and 1/4 cups all-purpose flour
- 1/2 cup unsalted butter, chilled and cut into small pieces
- 1/4 cup granulated sugar
- 1/4 teaspoon salt
- 3-4 tablespoons ice water

For the Coconut Cream Filling:

- 2 cups coconut milk (canned, full-fat)
- 1 cup whole milk
- 3/4 cup granulated sugar
- 1/3 cup cornstarch
- 1/4 teaspoon salt
- 4 large egg yolks
- 1 cup shredded coconut (sweetened or unsweetened)
- 2 tablespoons unsalted butter
- 1 teaspoon vanilla extract
- 1 cup whipped cream (for topping)

For Topping:

- 1 cup whipped cream
- 1/2 cup shredded coconut, toasted

Instructions:

Making the Pie Crust:

> In a food processor, combine the flour, sugar, and salt. Pulse to mix.
> Add the chilled butter to the processor and pulse until the mixture resembles coarse crumbs.
> Gradually add the ice water, one tablespoon at a time, and pulse until the dough just comes together.
> Turn the dough out onto a floured surface, knead it a few times to form a smooth ball, and then flatten it into a disk.

Wrap the dough in plastic wrap and refrigerate for at least 1 hour.
Preheat your oven to 375°F (190°C).
On a floured surface, roll out the chilled dough to fit a 9-inch pie pan.
Press the dough into the pan, trim any excess, and crimp the edges.
Prick the bottom of the crust with a fork and bake in the preheated oven for about 15 minutes or until lightly golden. Allow the crust to cool completely.

Making the Coconut Cream Filling:

In a saucepan, combine the coconut milk, whole milk, sugar, cornstarch, and salt. Whisk until well combined.
Place the saucepan over medium heat and bring the mixture to a simmer, stirring constantly.
In a separate bowl, whisk the egg yolks. Gradually add a small amount of the hot milk mixture to the egg yolks, whisking constantly to temper the eggs.
Pour the egg mixture back into the saucepan with the remaining milk mixture, continuing to whisk.
Cook the mixture over medium heat, stirring constantly, until it thickens.
Remove from heat and stir in the shredded coconut, butter, and vanilla extract.
Let the coconut cream filling cool slightly before pouring it into the cooled pie crust.
Refrigerate the pie for at least 2-4 hours or until the coconut cream is set.

Making the Whipped Cream Topping:

In a chilled bowl, whip the heavy cream until soft peaks form.
Optionally, sweeten the whipped cream with a little sugar to taste.

Topping the Pie:

Spread the whipped cream over the chilled coconut cream filling.
Toast shredded coconut in a dry skillet over medium heat until golden brown.
Sprinkle the toasted coconut over the whipped cream.
Slice and serve your delicious Coconut Cream Pie.

This Coconut Cream Pie is a delightful combination of a buttery crust, luscious coconut cream filling, and a light and fluffy whipped cream topping. It's a perfect dessert for coconut lovers and a great addition to any special occasion.

Tiramisu Pastries

Ingredients:

For the Filling:

- 1 cup mascarpone cheese, softened
- 1/2 cup heavy cream
- 1/2 cup powdered sugar
- 1 teaspoon vanilla extract

For the Coffee Soaking Syrup:

- 1/2 cup strong brewed coffee, cooled
- 2 tablespoons coffee liqueur (optional)
- 2 tablespoons sugar

Other Ingredients:

- Ladyfinger biscuits
- Cocoa powder, for dusting

Instructions:

Making the Filling:

In a mixing bowl, whisk together the mascarpone cheese, heavy cream, powdered sugar, and vanilla extract until smooth and well combined.
Adjust the sweetness to your liking by adding more powdered sugar if needed. Set aside.

Making the Coffee Soaking Syrup:

In a separate bowl, combine the strong brewed coffee, coffee liqueur (if using), and sugar. Stir until the sugar is dissolved.

Assembling the Tiramisu Pastries:

Dip each ladyfinger biscuit into the coffee soaking syrup, ensuring they are well-coated but not overly soggy.
Arrange a layer of soaked ladyfingers in the bottom of serving glasses or a serving dish.
Spoon a layer of the mascarpone filling over the ladyfingers.
Repeat the layers, finishing with a layer of the mascarpone filling on top.
Refrigerate the assembled pastries for at least 2-4 hours or overnight to allow the flavors to meld and the pastries to set.

Serving:
- Before serving, dust the tops of the Tiramisu Pastries with cocoa powder using a fine sieve.
- Optionally, garnish with chocolate shavings or a sprinkle of grated chocolate.
- Serve chilled and enjoy!

These Tiramisu Pastries capture the essence of the classic Tiramisu dessert in a convenient individual serving. They are perfect for entertaining or as a special treat for yourself. Feel free to get creative with the presentation and enjoy the rich and indulgent flavors of Tiramisu in pastry form.

Savory Pastries:

Spinach and Feta Puffs

Ingredients:

- 1 package (about 10 ounces) frozen chopped spinach, thawed and drained
- 1 cup crumbled feta cheese
- 1/2 cup grated Parmesan cheese
- 1/4 cup chopped green onions
- 2 cloves garlic, minced
- 1/4 teaspoon black pepper
- 1/4 teaspoon dried oregano
- 1/4 teaspoon dried thyme
- 1/4 teaspoon nutmeg
- 2 sheets puff pastry, thawed if frozen
- 1 egg, beaten (for egg wash)

Instructions:

Preparing the Filling:

>Preheat your oven to 400°F (200°C) and line a baking sheet with parchment paper.
>In a mixing bowl, combine the thawed and drained chopped spinach, crumbled feta cheese, grated Parmesan cheese, chopped green onions, minced garlic, black pepper, dried oregano, dried thyme, and nutmeg. Mix well to combine.

Assembling the Puffs:

>Roll out each sheet of puff pastry on a lightly floured surface to smooth out any creases.
>Cut each sheet into squares or rectangles, depending on your preference and the size you desire.
>Place a spoonful of the spinach and feta filling in the center of each pastry square.
>Fold the pastry over the filling to form a triangle or rectangle, depending on the shape you cut.
>Use a fork to crimp the edges of the pastry to seal the filling inside.
>Place the assembled puffs on the prepared baking sheet.

Baking:

>Brush the tops of the puff pastry with the beaten egg for a golden finish.

Bake in the preheated oven for 15-20 minutes or until the puffs are golden brown and puffed up.

Remove from the oven and let them cool slightly before serving.

Serving:

Serve the Spinach and Feta Puffs warm as a delightful appetizer or snack.

Optionally, garnish with additional chopped green onions or a sprinkle of Parmesan cheese.

These Spinach and Feta Puffs are a tasty and convenient way to enjoy the classic combination of spinach and feta in a flaky puff pastry. They make for a great addition to party platters or as a savory treat for any occasion.

Cheese and Herb Scones

Ingredients:

- 2 cups all-purpose flour
- 2 teaspoons baking powder
- 1/2 teaspoon baking soda
- 1/2 teaspoon salt
- 1/2 cup unsalted butter, cold and cubed
- 1 cup shredded sharp cheddar cheese
- 1 tablespoon fresh herbs (such as chives, parsley, or thyme), chopped
- 3/4 cup buttermilk
- 1 egg (for egg wash)

Instructions:

Preparing the Dough:

Preheat your oven to 425°F (220°C) and line a baking sheet with parchment paper.
In a large mixing bowl, whisk together the flour, baking powder, baking soda, and salt.
Add the cold, cubed butter to the dry ingredients. Use a pastry cutter or your fingertips to cut the butter into the flour until the mixture resembles coarse crumbs.
Stir in the shredded cheddar cheese and chopped fresh herbs until evenly distributed.
Make a well in the center of the mixture and pour in the buttermilk. Gently mix until just combined. Be careful not to overmix; the dough should be slightly sticky.

Shaping and Cutting:

Turn the dough out onto a floured surface and knead it lightly a few times until it comes together.
Pat the dough into a circle or rectangle about 1 inch (2.5 cm) thick.
Use a floured round cutter or a sharp knife to cut out scones from the dough.
Place the scones on the prepared baking sheet, leaving some space between each.

Baking:

In a small bowl, beat the egg to create an egg wash. Brush the tops of the scones with the egg wash.
Bake in the preheated oven for 12-15 minutes or until the scones are golden brown and cooked through.
Remove from the oven and let the scones cool on a wire rack.

Serving:

> Serve the Cheese and Herb Scones warm, either on their own or with a pat of butter. Enjoy them as a side for soups, salads, or as a savory snack.

These Cheese and Herb Scones are flaky, cheesy, and packed with aromatic herbs. They make for a delightful addition to your brunch or afternoon tea. Customize the herbs based on your preferences for a personalized touch.

Tomato and Mozzarella Galette

Ingredients:

For the Galette Dough:

- 1 and 1/4 cups all-purpose flour
- 1/2 teaspoon salt
- 1/2 cup unsalted butter, cold and cut into small cubes
- 1/4 cup ice water

For the Filling:

- 4-5 medium-sized tomatoes, thinly sliced
- 8 ounces fresh mozzarella cheese, sliced
- 2 tablespoons olive oil
- 2 tablespoons balsamic glaze (optional)
- 1/4 cup fresh basil leaves, chopped
- Salt and pepper to taste

Instructions:

Making the Galette Dough:

In a food processor, combine the flour and salt. Add the cold, cubed butter and pulse until the mixture resembles coarse crumbs.
Gradually add the ice water, one tablespoon at a time, pulsing until the dough just comes together.
Turn the dough out onto a floured surface, knead it a few times, and shape it into a disk. Wrap the disk in plastic wrap and refrigerate for at least 30 minutes.

Assembling the Galette:

Preheat your oven to 375°F (190°C) and line a baking sheet with parchment paper.
On a floured surface, roll out the chilled dough into a circle about 12 inches (30 cm) in diameter.
Transfer the rolled-out dough to the prepared baking sheet.
Arrange the sliced mozzarella over the center of the dough, leaving a border around the edges.
Layer the thinly sliced tomatoes over the mozzarella.

Drizzle the olive oil over the tomatoes and mozzarella. Season with salt and pepper to taste.

Fold the edges of the dough over the filling, pleating as you go to create a rustic look.

Bake in the preheated oven for 30-35 minutes or until the crust is golden brown.

Finishing Touches:

Remove the galette from the oven and let it cool slightly.

Drizzle balsamic glaze over the top if desired.

Sprinkle chopped fresh basil over the galette just before serving.

Slice and enjoy your Tomato and Mozzarella Galette warm.

This Tomato and Mozzarella Galette is a wonderful way to showcase the vibrant flavors of summer tomatoes and the creaminess of fresh mozzarella. It's a versatile dish that can be served as an appetizer, a light lunch, or a flavorful side dish.

Bacon and Cheddar Pinwheels

Ingredients:

- 1 sheet puff pastry, thawed if frozen
- 6 slices bacon, cooked and crumbled
- 1 cup shredded cheddar cheese
- 1/4 cup green onions, finely chopped
- 1/4 cup mayonnaise
- 1 teaspoon Dijon mustard
- 1/2 teaspoon garlic powder
- Salt and pepper to taste
- 1 egg (for egg wash)

Instructions:

Preparing the Filling:

In a bowl, combine the crumbled bacon, shredded cheddar cheese, chopped green onions, mayonnaise, Dijon mustard, garlic powder, salt, and pepper. Mix well until all ingredients are evenly incorporated.

Assembling the Pinwheels:

Preheat your oven to 400°F (200°C) and line a baking sheet with parchment paper.
Roll out the puff pastry sheet on a lightly floured surface to smooth out any creases.
Spread the bacon and cheddar filling evenly over the entire surface of the puff pastry.
Starting from one edge, tightly roll the puff pastry sheet into a log or cylinder.
Brush the edge of the pastry with a little water to help seal the roll.
Place the rolled puff pastry in the refrigerator for about 15-20 minutes to firm up slightly, making it easier to slice.

Slicing and Baking:

Remove the chilled roll from the refrigerator and slice it into 1/2-inch thick pinwheels.
Place the pinwheels on the prepared baking sheet, leaving some space between each.

In a small bowl, beat the egg to create an egg wash. Brush the tops of the pinwheels with the egg wash for a golden finish.

Bake in the preheated oven for 12-15 minutes or until the pinwheels are puffed up and golden brown.

Remove from the oven and let them cool slightly before serving.

Serving:

Serve the Bacon and Cheddar Pinwheels warm as a delicious appetizer or snack. Optionally, garnish with additional chopped green onions or serve with a dipping sauce of your choice.

These Bacon and Cheddar Pinwheels are a crowd-pleaser, combining the irresistible flavors of bacon and cheddar in a flaky and buttery puff pastry. They are quick to make and disappear even faster when served at parties or gatherings.

Chicken Pot Pie

Ingredients:

For the Pie Filling:

- 1/3 cup unsalted butter
- 1/3 cup all-purpose flour
- 1/2 teaspoon salt
- 1/4 teaspoon black pepper
- 1/4 teaspoon celery seed
- 1/4 teaspoon onion powder
- 1/4 teaspoon garlic powder
- 1/4 teaspoon dried thyme
- 1 and 3/4 cups chicken broth
- 2/3 cup milk
- 2 cups cooked chicken, shredded or diced
- 1 cup frozen mixed vegetables (peas, carrots, corn, and green beans)

For the Pie Crust:

- 2 store-bought or homemade pie crusts (enough for a top and bottom crust)

Instructions:

Preparing the Pie Filling:

Preheat your oven to 425°F (220°C).
In a large saucepan, melt the butter over medium heat. Add the flour, salt, pepper, celery seed, onion powder, garlic powder, and dried thyme. Stir continuously until the mixture becomes a smooth paste.
Gradually whisk in the chicken broth and milk, stirring constantly to avoid lumps.
Continue cooking and stirring until the mixture thickens.
Add the cooked chicken and frozen mixed vegetables to the sauce, stirring to combine. Remove from heat.

Assembling the Chicken Pot Pie:

Roll out one pie crust and place it in the bottom of a 9-inch pie dish.
Pour the chicken and vegetable filling into the pie crust.
Roll out the second pie crust and place it on top of the filling. Seal the edges and crimp with a fork or your fingers.

Cut a few slits in the top crust to allow steam to escape during baking.

Baking:

Place the pie dish on a baking sheet to catch any potential spills.
Bake in the preheated oven for 30-35 minutes or until the crust is golden brown and the filling is bubbly.
If the crust edges start to brown too quickly, you can cover them with aluminum foil.
Remove from the oven and let the Chicken Pot Pie cool for a few minutes before serving.

Serving:

Slice and serve the Chicken Pot Pie while it's warm and comforting.
Enjoy this classic dish on its own or with a side of salad for a complete meal.

This Chicken Pot Pie recipe is a perfect way to enjoy the comforting flavors of a homey, classic dish. It's a great option for family dinners or whenever you're craving a hearty and satisfying meal.

Sausage Rolls

Ingredients:

- 1 pound (about 450g) ground sausage meat (pork or a combination of pork and beef)
- 1 onion, finely chopped
- 2 cloves garlic, minced
- 1 cup breadcrumbs
- 1/4 cup parsley, chopped
- Salt and pepper to taste
- 2 sheets puff pastry, thawed if frozen
- 1 egg (for egg wash)

Instructions:

Preparing the Sausage Filling:

Preheat your oven to 400°F (200°C) and line a baking sheet with parchment paper.

In a large mixing bowl, combine the ground sausage meat, chopped onion, minced garlic, breadcrumbs, chopped parsley, salt, and pepper. Mix well until all the ingredients are evenly incorporated.

Assembling the Sausage Rolls:

Roll out the puff pastry sheets on a lightly floured surface to smooth out any creases.
Divide the sausage mixture into two portions.
Place one portion of the sausage mixture along the center of each puff pastry sheet in a log shape.
Fold one side of the puff pastry over the sausage mixture, followed by the other side, so the sausage is completely enclosed.
Press the edges to seal the seam, and place the rolls seam-side down.

Slicing and Baking:

Beat the egg in a small bowl to create an egg wash.
Brush the tops of the sausage rolls with the egg wash for a golden finish.
Use a sharp knife to slice each roll into smaller individual rolls, about 2 inches in length.
Place the sausage rolls on the prepared baking sheet.
Bake in the preheated oven for 20-25 minutes or until the pastry is golden brown and the sausage is cooked through.

Serving:

Remove from the oven and let the sausage rolls cool slightly before serving.
Serve the Sausage Rolls warm on their own or with your favorite dipping sauce.

Sausage rolls are a versatile and crowd-pleasing snack or appetizer. They are great for parties, picnics, or as a tasty addition to your meal. Enjoy the flaky puff pastry and flavorful sausage filling in every bite!

Specialty Pastries:

Kouign-Amann

Ingredients:

For the Dough:

- 2 1/4 teaspoons (1 packet) active dry yeast
- 1 cup lukewarm water
- 2 3/4 cups all-purpose flour, plus extra for dusting
- 1 teaspoon salt
- 1 cup (2 sticks) unsalted butter, cold

For the Butter Block:

- 1 cup (2 sticks) unsalted butter, softened
- 1 cup granulated sugar

For Assembly:

- Additional granulated sugar for dusting

Instructions:

Making the Dough:

> In a small bowl, dissolve the active dry yeast in lukewarm water. Let it sit for about 5 minutes until it becomes frothy.
> In a large mixing bowl, combine the flour and salt. Add the yeast mixture and mix until a dough forms.
> Knead the dough on a floured surface until it becomes smooth. Shape it into a rectangle, cover with plastic wrap, and refrigerate for 30 minutes.

Preparing the Butter Block:

> Place the softened butter and granulated sugar in a bowl. Mix until well combined.
> Roll out the butter-sugar mixture between two sheets of parchment paper into a rectangle that is approximately the same size as the chilled dough.
> Place the butter block in the refrigerator for about 15 minutes to firm up.

Assembling the Kouign-Amann:

- Roll out the chilled dough on a floured surface into a larger rectangle.
- Place the chilled butter block on two-thirds of the dough, leaving one-third of the dough uncovered.
- Fold the uncovered third over the middle third, then fold the remaining third on top, creating layers.
- Roll out the folded dough again into a rectangle.
- Repeat the folding process (known as "turns") a total of three times, chilling the dough in the refrigerator between each turn.
- After the final turn, roll out the dough into a large rectangle.
- Sprinkle the surface with granulated sugar and fold it into thirds.
- Cut the folded dough into squares or rectangles.

Baking:

- Preheat your oven to 375°F (190°C).
- Place the Kouign-Amann pieces in muffin cups or on a lined baking sheet.
- Bake in the preheated oven for about 25-30 minutes or until the pastries are golden brown and caramelized.
- Remove from the oven and let them cool slightly before serving.

Serving:

- Serve the Kouign-Amann warm and enjoy the layers of flaky, caramelized goodness.
- Dust with additional sugar if desired.

Kouign-Amann is a delicious treat that combines the richness of butter with layers of sugar and dough, resulting in a pastry with a crispy, caramelized exterior and a soft, flaky interior. It's a delightful indulgence for any pastry lover.

Mango Coconut Turnovers

Ingredients:

For the Filling:

- 2 cups ripe mango, diced
- 1/2 cup shredded coconut (sweetened or unsweetened)
- 1/4 cup granulated sugar
- 1 tablespoon cornstarch
- 1 teaspoon lime juice
- Pinch of salt

For the Turnovers:

- 1 package (17.3 ounces) puff pastry sheets, thawed if frozen
- 1 egg, beaten (for egg wash)
- Powdered sugar for dusting (optional)

Instructions:

Making the Filling:

In a bowl, combine the diced mango, shredded coconut, granulated sugar, cornstarch, lime juice, and a pinch of salt. Mix well to coat the mango evenly. Allow the filling mixture to sit for a few minutes to let the flavors meld.

Assembling the Turnovers:

Preheat your oven to the temperature specified on the puff pastry package (usually around 400°F or 200°C). Line a baking sheet with parchment paper.
Roll out the puff pastry sheets on a lightly floured surface.
Cut each puff pastry sheet into squares or rectangles, depending on your preference and the size you desire for the turnovers.
Place a spoonful of the mango-coconut filling in the center of each pastry square.
Fold the pastry over the filling to create a triangle or rectangle shape. Press the edges to seal, and use a fork to crimp the edges for a decorative touch.
Place the turnovers on the prepared baking sheet.

Baking:

Brush the tops of the turnovers with beaten egg to create a golden finish.

Bake in the preheated oven according to the puff pastry package instructions or until the turnovers are puffed up and golden brown.
Remove from the oven and let them cool slightly.

Serving:

Dust the Mango Coconut Turnovers with powdered sugar if desired.
Serve warm and enjoy the tropical flavors.

These Mango Coconut Turnovers are a perfect treat for breakfast, brunch, or as a sweet snack. The combination of juicy mango and sweet coconut encased in flaky puff pastry creates a delightful pastry that's sure to be a hit.

Raspberry Pistachio Bostock

Ingredients:

For the Syrup:

- 1/2 cup water
- 1/2 cup granulated sugar
- 1 tablespoon raspberry liqueur (optional)
- 1 teaspoon vanilla extract

For the Almond Cream:

- 1/2 cup unsalted butter, softened
- 1/2 cup granulated sugar
- 1 cup almond flour
- 1 teaspoon vanilla extract
- 2 large eggs

For Assembly:

- Slices of brioche bread
- Raspberry jam or preserves
- Fresh raspberries
- Chopped pistachios

Instructions:

Making the Syrup:

In a small saucepan, combine water and granulated sugar. Bring to a simmer over medium heat, stirring until the sugar is dissolved.
Remove from heat and let it cool slightly. Stir in the raspberry liqueur (if using) and vanilla extract.

Making the Almond Cream:

In a bowl, cream together the softened butter and granulated sugar until light and fluffy.
Add almond flour and vanilla extract to the butter mixture, mixing well.
Beat in the eggs one at a time until the almond cream is smooth and well combined.

Assembling the Bostock:

Preheat your oven to 375°F (190°C). Line a baking sheet with parchment paper.

Dip each slice of brioche into the prepared syrup, ensuring it's coated on both sides.
Place the soaked slices on the baking sheet.
Spread a layer of raspberry jam or preserves over each brioche slice.
Spoon a generous amount of almond cream over the raspberry jam.
Scatter fresh raspberries and chopped pistachios over the almond cream.

Baking:

Bake in the preheated oven for about 15-20 minutes or until the almond cream is set and golden brown.
Remove from the oven and let the Raspberry Pistachio Bostock cool slightly.

Serving:

Serve the Bostock warm or at room temperature.
Optionally, dust with powdered sugar before serving.

Raspberry Pistachio Bostock is a luxurious and flavorful pastry, perfect for brunch or a special breakfast treat. The combination of almond cream, raspberries, and pistachios creates a delightful balance of flavors and textures.

Matcha Swirl Buns

Ingredients:

For the Dough:

- 3 1/2 cups all-purpose flour
- 1/3 cup granulated sugar
- 2 1/4 teaspoons active dry yeast (1 packet)
- 1 teaspoon matcha powder
- 1 cup warm milk
- 1/4 cup unsalted butter, melted
- 1/2 teaspoon salt
- 1 large egg

For the Matcha Swirl Filling:

- 2 tablespoons matcha powder
- 1/4 cup granulated sugar
- 2 tablespoons unsalted butter, softened

For the Glaze:

- 1 cup powdered sugar
- 1-2 tablespoons milk
- 1/2 teaspoon matcha powder (optional, for color)

Instructions:

Making the Dough:

In a small bowl, combine warm milk and sugar. Sprinkle the yeast over the mixture and let it sit for about 5 minutes until it becomes frothy.
In a large mixing bowl, whisk together the flour, matcha powder, and salt.
Make a well in the center of the flour mixture and add the yeast mixture, melted butter, and beaten egg.
Mix the ingredients until a dough forms.
Knead the dough on a floured surface for about 8-10 minutes until it becomes smooth and elastic.
Place the dough in a greased bowl, cover with a kitchen towel, and let it rise in a warm place for about 1-1.5 hours, or until it doubles in size.

Making the Matcha Swirl Filling:

In a small bowl, mix together matcha powder, granulated sugar, and softened butter until well combined.

Assembling the Buns:

Punch down the risen dough and roll it out on a floured surface into a rectangle.
Spread the matcha swirl filling evenly over the surface of the dough.
Roll the dough tightly from one end to form a log.
Cut the log into equal-sized slices to make individual buns.
Place the buns in a greased baking pan, leaving some space between each.
Cover the pan with a kitchen towel and let the buns rise for another 30-45 minutes.

Baking:

Preheat your oven to 375°F (190°C).
Bake the Matcha Swirl Buns in the preheated oven for about 15-20 minutes or until they are golden brown.
Remove from the oven and let the buns cool slightly.

Making the Glaze:

In a bowl, whisk together powdered sugar and milk until smooth.
If desired, add matcha powder to a portion of the glaze for a green color.

Glazing:

Drizzle the glaze over the warm Matcha Swirl Buns.
Allow the glaze to set before serving.

These Matcha Swirl Buns are a delightful combination of soft, fluffy dough and a sweet matcha filling. Enjoy them as a delicious breakfast or snack with a cup of tea or coffee.

Fig and Goat Cheese Tart

Ingredients:

For the Tart Crust:

- 1 1/2 cups all-purpose flour
- 1/2 cup unsalted butter, chilled and cubed
- 1/4 cup granulated sugar
- 1/4 teaspoon salt
- 2-3 tablespoons ice water

For the Filling:

- 8 ounces goat cheese, softened
- 1/4 cup honey
- 1 teaspoon vanilla extract

For Topping:

- Fresh figs, sliced
- Honey, for drizzling
- Fresh thyme leaves (optional, for garnish)

Instructions:

Making the Tart Crust:

In a food processor, combine the flour, sugar, and salt. Pulse a few times to mix.
Add the chilled, cubed butter to the flour mixture. Pulse until the mixture resembles coarse crumbs.
With the food processor running, add ice water one tablespoon at a time until the dough comes together. Be careful not to over-process.
Turn the dough out onto a lightly floured surface. Gather it into a ball, flatten it into a disc, and wrap it in plastic wrap. Chill in the refrigerator for at least 30 minutes.
Preheat your oven to 375°F (190°C).
Roll out the chilled dough on a floured surface to fit a tart pan. Press the dough into the pan, trimming any excess.
Line the crust with parchment paper and fill it with pie weights or dried beans. Blind bake the crust for about 15 minutes. Remove the weights and parchment, then bake for an additional 5-7 minutes or until the crust is golden brown. Allow it to cool.

Making the Goat Cheese Filling:

In a bowl, mix together the softened goat cheese, honey, and vanilla extract until well combined and smooth.

Assembling the Tart:

Spread the goat cheese mixture evenly over the cooled tart crust.
Arrange the sliced figs on top of the goat cheese.
Drizzle honey over the figs for added sweetness.
Optional: Garnish with fresh thyme leaves for a pop of color and flavor.

Serving:

Slice and serve the Fig and Goat Cheese Tart at room temperature.
Enjoy as a delightful dessert or appetizer.

This Fig and Goat Cheese Tart is a perfect balance of sweet and savory, making it an elegant and delicious treat. The combination of fresh figs, creamy goat cheese, and a buttery crust creates a delightful flavor profile that is sure to impress.

www.ingramcontent.com/pod-product-compliance
Lightning Source LLC
LaVergne TN
LVHW081603060526
838201LV00054B/2054